RECKONER

The Diagram Group

The publishers wish to
thank all those who helped
in the preparation of this book

A Diagram book created by Diagram
Information and edited by the Diagram
Group

First published 1990

© Diagram Visual Information Limited 1990

All rights reserved
No part of this publication...

HarperCollinsPublishers

HarperCollins Publishers
P.O. Box, Glasgow G4 0NB

A Diagram book first created by Diagram Visual
Information Limited of 195 Kentish Town Road,
London NW5 8SY

First published 1995

Reprint 10 9 8 7 6 5 4 3 2 1 0

ISBN 0 00 470851 2

Printed in Great Britain by
HarperCollins Manufacturing, Glasgow

Introduction

What is the decimal equivalent of ⅛? What quantity of food is needed for a party of six people? How is turf laid? These and many other questions are answered in *Collins Gem Home Reckoner*. Problems and queries concerning domestic realms as diverse as the garden and the kitchen, decorating and fabric care are examined, explained and resolved.

This volume contains handy tips on a variety of topics in easy-to-follow steps. How to plan a garden or a tile arrangement, how to calculate the amount of paint needed to decorate a room, a comprehensive list of foods and their calorie content, and much more are included. For weights and measures in the home and garden, metric and imperial unit conversion tables are provided; they give both approximate or 'handy' equivalents and exact ones.

With its collection of conversion tables, providing immediate visual reference, and its clear step-by-step instructions, the *Collins Gem Home Reckoner* is an invaluable companion in both the home and the garden.

4

Contents

4. Decorating and DIY

5. In the garden

Chart and table finder

1. Home mathematical problems

USING A CALCULATOR

The basic keys

ON/C This key switches on the calculator. When the calculator is already on, pressing this key clears the display. Some (solar-powered) calculators do not have an ON key. The C key may be labelled 'AC', for all clear, instead.

OFF This switches off the calculator.

0 - 9 The number entry keys: pressing one of these enters the appropriate number on the display.

. The decimal point key. Pressing this enters a decimal point on the display.

CE Pressing this clears the last entry in a calculation. This function key may be labelled 'C' on some calculators.

+ −
× ÷ These keys allow you to perform the four basic arithmetic functions: addition (+), subtraction (−), multiplication (×) and division (÷).

= The equals key: this gives the result of a calculation.

M+ This key adds the display number to the memory.

M− This key subtracts the display number from the memory.

RM This 'memory recall' key displays the contents of the memory. This function key may be labelled 'MR' on some calculators.

CM This key clears the memory. Some calculators do not have this function or the key, if there, may be labelled 'MC'.

% This key calculates percentages.

√ This key calculates the square root of the display number.

Calculator display and keys

SIMPLE CALCULATIONS
Addition

To perform the calculation **36 + 57**, press the calculator keys in the following sequence:

	Press key	Display shows
1	ON/C	0. (screen ready)
2	3	3.
3	6	36.
4	+	36. +
5	5	5. +
6	7	57. +
7	=	93. (the answer)

Notes: At any stage in a calculation you can press the = key. This will give you the sum up to the stage you have reached. You can then continue with your calculation.

Not all calculators display the +, −, × and ÷ symbols shown here and on the following pages.

To perform a calculation that includes decimal points, such as **23.8 + 36.4**, press the calculator keys in the following sequence:

	Press key	Display shows
1	ON/C	0. (screen ready)
2	2	2.
3	3	23.
4	.	23.
5	8	23.8
6	+	23.8 +
7	3	3. +
8	6	36. +
9	.	36. +
10	4	36.4 +
11	=	60.2 (the answer)

Using the above examples as a guide, calculate the sums that follow. The answers are given at the bottom of the page.

1 72 + 31 + 54
2 13 + 49 + 191
3 13.3 + 14.9 + 19.8

Answers: **1** 157   **2** 253   **3** 48.0

Subtraction

To perform the calculation **33 + 48 – 17**, press the calculator keys in the following sequence:

	Press key	Display shows
1	ON/C	0. (screen ready)
2	3	3.
3	3	33.
4	+	33. +
5	4	4. +
6	8	48. +
7	–	81. – (the sum so far)
8	1	1.
9	7	17.
10	=	64. (the answer)

Using the above example as a guide, calculate the sums that follow. The answers are given at the bottom of the page.

$$1 \ 22 + 47 - 19$$
$$2 \ 43 - 17 + 11$$
$$3 \ 11.3 - 14.9 + 12.1$$

Answers: **1** 50   **2** 37   **3** 8.5

Multiplication

To perform the calculation **33 × 24**, simply press the calculator keys in the order of the sum from left to right. The sequence of keys is as follows:

	Press key	Display shows
1	ON/C	0. (screen ready)
2	3	3.
3	3	33.
4	×	33. ×
5	2	2. ×
6	4	24. ×
7	=	792. (the answer)

Using the above example as a guide, calculate the sums that follow. The answers are given below the sums.

$$1\ 12 \times 47$$
$$2\ 43 \times 13 \times 11$$
$$3\ 11.9 \times 14.3$$

Answers: **1** 564   **2** 6149   **3** 170.17

Division

To perform the calculation **156 ÷ 13**, simply press the calculator keys in the order of the sum from left to right. The sequence of keys is as follows overleaf:

	Press key	Display shows
1	ON/C	0. (screen ready)
2	1	1.
3	5	15.
4	6	156.
5	÷	156.÷
6	1	1.÷
7	3	13.÷
8	=	12. (the answer)

Using the above example as a guide, calculate the sums that follow. The answers are given below the sums.

1 414 ÷ 9
2 988 ÷ 13
3 98 ÷ 28

Answers: **1** 46   **2** 76   **3** 3.5

Percentages

'Per cent' means 'out of one hundred'. The symbol for per cent is %.

There are many occasions in everyday life when you may need to work out a percentage. For example, in an end-of-season sale you may need to decide from which store to purchase a washing machine. At store A, the normal price of the washing machine is £450, and in the sale it is reduced by 12%. In store B, the same model is normally £475, but in the sale it is reduced by 15%. Which store has the cheaper sale price for the washing machine?

There are two ways of calculating this, depending whether or not your calculator has a % key.

Percentages for calculators with a % key To work out 12% of £450, you multiply 450 by 12%. 12% of £450 then becomes $450 \times 12\%$

The key sequence for this is:

	Press key	Display shows
1	ON/C	0.
2	4	4.
3	5	45.
4	0	450.
5	×	450. ×
6	1	1. ×
7	2	12. ×
8	%	54. (the answer)

This gives you by how much the item is reduced. To work out the sale price of the item you need to subtract this from the original amount. So to complete the sum, press the keys shown overleaf (not all calculators display the M, for memory):

	Press key	Display shows
9	MC	54. (memory cleared)
10	M+	M54. (54 added to memory)
11	4	M4.
12	5	M45.
13	0	M450.
14	−	M450. −
15	RM	M54. −(54 recalled from memory)
16	=	M396. (the answer)

Using the above example as a guide, in the same way calculate 15% of £475 and then work out the sale price of the item at store B. At which store is the item cheaper? (The answer is at the bottom of p. 19.)

Percentages for calculators without a % key To work out 12% of £450, you change the percentage into a fraction. Remember, 'per cent' means 'out of a hundred', so to change the percentage to a fraction you divide by 100. So 12% of £450 is:

$$\frac{12}{100} \times 450$$

The key sequence for this is given on the opposite page.

This gives you by how much the item is reduced. To work out the sale price of the item you need to subtract this from the original amount. So to complete the sum,

	Press key	Display shows
1	ON/C	0.
2	1	1.
3	2	12.
4	÷	12.÷
5	1	1.÷
6	0	10.÷
7	0	100.÷
8	=	0.12
9	×	0.12 ×
10	4	4.×
11	5	45.×
12	0	450.×
13	=	54. (the answer)

press the the sequence of keys (from 9 to 16) shown on p. 18.

Using this example as a guide, in the same way calculate 15% of £475 and then work out the sale price of the item at store B. At which store is the item cheaper? (The answer is at the bottom of the page.)

Answer: At store B the item is £403.75. So, the item is cheaper at store A, where it is £396.00.

EASY MULTIPLICATION

For some problems of multiplication there are easy solutions, depending on the number you are multiplying by. These are useful if you do not have a calculator available. You can easily convert difficult multiplication to easy addition or subtraction.

Multiplication by 1, 10, 100, etc.
When multiplying by 1, you get the same number (**a**).
When multiplying by 10, simply put a 0 on the end of the number you are multiplying (**b**).
When multiplying by 100 simply put two 0s on the end of the number you are multiplying (**c**).

$$\textbf{a } 275 \times 1 = 275$$
$$\textbf{b } 275 \times 10 = 2750$$
$$\textbf{c } 275 \times 100 = 27\,500$$

Multiplying by 2
When multiplying by 2, just add the number to itself, a simple matter of addition (**d**).

$$\textbf{d } 275 \times 2 \longrightarrow \begin{array}{r} 275 \\ + 275 \\ \hline 550 \end{array}$$

Multiplying by 5
When multiplying by 5, simply put a 0 on the end of the number you are multiplying and then divide that number by 2 (**e**).

$$\textbf{e } 426 \times 5 \longrightarrow \begin{array}{r} 2\overline{)4260} \\ \hline 2130 \end{array}$$

Multiplying by 9
When multiplying by 9, simply put a 0 on the end of
the number you are multiplying and then subtract that
original number from the other (**f**).

$$
\begin{array}{r}
\textbf{f } 275 \times 9 \rightarrow 2750 \\
- 275 \\
\hline
2475
\end{array}
$$

Multiplying by 11
When multiplying by 11, simply put a 0 on the end of
the number you are multiplying and then add that
original number to the other (**g**).

$$
\begin{array}{r}
\textbf{g } 426 \times 11 \rightarrow 4260 \\
+ 426 \\
\hline
4686
\end{array}
$$

Multiplying by 15
When multiplying by 15, simply put a 0 on the end of
the number you are multiplying, then divide this
number in half, and add the two together (**h**).

$$
\textbf{h } 426 \times 15 \rightarrow 4260 \rightarrow 2)\dfrac{4260}{2130} \rightarrow \begin{array}{r} 4260 \\ + 2130 \\ \hline 6390 \end{array}
$$

Multiplying by 19
When multiplying by 19, simply multiply by 2, put a 0
on the end of this total, and then subtract the original
number from the total (**i**).

$$
\textbf{i } 426 \times 19 \rightarrow \begin{array}{r} 426 \\ \times 2 \\ \hline 852 \end{array} \rightarrow \begin{array}{r} 8520 \\ - 426 \\ \hline 8094 \end{array}
$$

3×5
4×5
5×5
MULTIPLICATION TABLES
The tables below give you all the answers you
will need when multiplying numbers 1 to 95 by
numbers 2 to 6.

×2		×3		×4		×5		×6	
1	2	1	3	1	4	1	5	1	6
2	4	2	6	2	8	2	10	2	12
3	6	3	9	3	12	3	15	3	18
4	8	4	12	4	16	4	20	4	24
5	10	5	15	5	20	5	25	5	30
6	12	6	18	6	24	6	30	6	36
7	14	7	21	7	28	7	35	7	42
8	16	8	24	8	32	8	40	8	48
9	18	9	27	9	36	9	45	9	54
10	20	10	30	10	40	10	50	10	60
11	22	11	33	11	44	11	55	11	66
12	24	12	36	12	48	12	60	12	72
13	26	13	39	13	52	13	65	13	78
14	28	14	42	14	56	14	70	14	84
15	30	15	45	15	60	15	75	15	90
16	32	16	48	16	64	16	80	16	96
17	34	17	51	17	68	17	85	17	102
18	36	18	54	18	72	18	90	18	108
19	38	19	57	19	76	19	95	19	114
25	50	25	75	25	100	25	125	25	150
35	70	35	105	35	140	35	175	35	210
45	90	45	135	45	180	45	225	45	270
55	110	55	165	55	220	55	275	55	330
65	130	65	195	65	260	65	325	65	390
75	150	75	225	75	300	75	375	75	450
85	170	85	255	85	340	85	425	85	510
95	190	95	285	95	380	95	475	95	570

The tables below give you all the answers you will need
when multiplying numbers 1 to 95 by numbers 7 to 11.

×7		×8		×9		×10		×11	
1	7	1	8	1	9	1	10	1	11
2	14	2	16	2	18	2	20	2	22
3	21	3	24	3	27	3	30	3	33
4	28	4	32	4	36	4	40	4	44
5	35	5	40	5	45	5	50	5	55
6	42	6	48	6	54	6	60	6	66
7	49	7	56	7	63	7	70	7	77
8	56	8	64	8	72	8	80	8	88
9	63	9	72	9	81	9	90	9	99
10	70	10	80	10	90	10	100	10	110
11	77	11	88	11	99	11	110	11	121
12	84	12	96	12	108	12	120	12	132
13	91	13	104	13	117	13	130	13	143
14	98	14	112	14	126	14	140	14	154
15	105	15	120	15	135	15	150	15	165
16	112	16	128	16	144	16	160	16	176
17	119	17	136	17	153	17	170	17	187
18	126	18	144	18	162	18	180	18	198
19	133	19	152	19	171	19	190	19	209
25	175	25	200	25	225	25	250	25	275
35	245	35	280	35	315	35	350	35	385
45	315	45	360	45	405	45	450	45	495
55	385	55	440	55	495	55	550	55	605
65	455	65	520	65	585	65	650	65	715
75	525	75	600	75	675	75	750	75	825
85	595	85	680	85	765	85	850	85	935
95	665	95	760	95	855	95	950	95	1045

The tables below give you all the answers you will
need when multiplying numbers 1 to 95 by numbers
12 to 16.

×12		×13		×14		×15		×16	
1	12	1	13	1	14	1	15	1	16
2	24	2	26	2	28	2	30	2	32
3	36	3	39	3	42	3	45	3	48
4	48	4	52	4	56	4	60	4	64
5	60	5	65	5	70	5	75	5	80
6	72	6	78	6	84	6	90	6	96
7	84	7	91	7	98	7	105	7	112
8	96	8	104	8	112	8	120	8	128
9	108	9	117	9	126	9	135	9	144
10	120	10	130	10	140	10	150	10	160
11	132	11	143	11	154	11	165	11	176
12	144	12	156	12	168	12	180	12	192
13	156	13	169	13	182	13	195	13	208
14	168	14	182	14	196	14	210	14	224
15	180	15	195	15	210	15	225	15	240
16	192	16	208	16	224	16	240	16	256
17	204	17	221	17	238	17	255	17	272
18	216	18	234	18	252	18	270	18	288
19	228	19	247	19	266	19	285	19	304
25	300	25	325	25	350	25	375	25	400
35	420	35	455	35	490	35	525	35	560
45	540	45	585	45	630	45	675	45	720
55	660	55	715	55	770	55	825	55	880
65	780	65	845	65	910	65	975	65	1040
75	900	75	975	75	1050	75	1125	75	1200
85	1020	85	1105	85	1190	85	1275	85	1360
95	1140	95	1235	95	1330	95	1425	95	1520

The tables below give you all the answers you will
need when multiplying numbers 1 to 95 by numbers
17 to 21.

×17		×18		×19		×20		×21	
1	17	1	18	1	19	1	20	1	21
2	34	2	36	2	38	2	40	2	42
3	51	3	54	3	57	3	60	3	63
4	68	4	72	4	76	4	80	4	84
5	85	5	90	5	95	5	100	5	105
6	102	6	108	6	114	6	120	6	126
7	119	7	126	7	133	7	140	7	147
8	136	8	144	8	152	8	160	8	168
9	153	9	162	9	171	9	180	9	189
10	170	10	180	10	190	10	200	10	210
11	187	11	198	11	209	11	220	11	231
12	204	12	216	12	228	12	240	12	252
13	221	13	234	13	247	13	260	13	273
14	238	14	252	14	266	14	280	14	294
15	255	15	270	15	285	15	300	15	315
16	272	16	288	16	304	16	320	16	336
17	289	17	306	17	323	17	340	17	357
18	306	18	324	18	342	18	360	18	378
19	323	19	342	19	361	19	380	19	399
25	425	25	450	25	475	25	500	25	525
35	595	35	630	35	665	35	700	35	735
45	765	45	810	45	855	45	900	45	945
55	935	55	990	55	1045	55	1100	55	1155
65	1105	65	1170	65	1235	65	1300	65	1365
75	1275	75	1350	75	1425	75	1500	75	1575
85	1445	85	1530	85	1615	85	1700	85	1785
95	1615	95	1710	95	1805	95	1900	95	1995

FRACTIONS, DECIMALS & PERCENTAGES

On pp. 27–30, fractions are shown with their decimal and percentage equivalents.

Fractions are shown as two numbers; one appears above a line and the other appears below. The number above the line is called the numerator and the one below it is the denominator. To find a fraction's decimal equivalent, you divide the numerator by the denominator.

In the table on the opposite page, all fractions whose numerator is 1 are listed (from ½ to ¹⁄₂₅). To find others, multiply the decimal by the new numerator. For example:

$$\tfrac{1}{8} = 0.125 = 12.50\%$$

To find ⅖, multiply by 2:

$$2 \times 0.125 = 0.25$$
$$\text{so}$$
$$\tfrac{2}{8} = 0.25 = 25\%$$

To find ⅜, multiply by 3:

$$3 \times 0.125 = 0.375$$
$$\text{so}$$
$$\tfrac{3}{8} = 0.375 = 37.5\%$$

Fractions with 1 as numerator

Fraction	Decimal	Percentage
$1/2$	0.5	50.00%
$1/3$	0.333 333	33.33%
$1/4$	0.25	25.00%
$1/5$	0.2	20.00%
$1/6$	0.166 667	16.67%
$1/7$	0.142 857	14.29%
$1/8$	0.125	12.50%
$1/9$	0.111 111	11.11%
$1/10$	0.1	10.00%
$1/11$	0.090 909	9.09%
$1/12$	0.083 333	8.33%
$1/13$	0.076 923	7.69%
$1/14$	0.071 428	7.14%
$1/15$	0.066 666	6.66%
$1/16$	0.062 5	6.25%
$1/20$	0.05	5.00%
$1/25$	0.04	4.00%

The 64ths table

Fraction	Decimal	Percentage
$1/64$	0.015 625	1.56%
$2/64 = 1/32$	0.031 25	3.13%
$3/64$	0.046 875	4.69%
$4/64 = 2/32 = 1/16$	0.062 5	6.25%
$5/64$	0.078 125	7.81%
$6/64 = 3/32$	0.093 75	9.38%
$7/64$	0.109 375	10.94%
$8/64 = 4/32 = 2/16 = 1/8$	0.125	12.50%
$9/64$	0.140 625	14.06%
$10/64 = 5/32$	0.156 25	15.63%
$11/64$	0.171 875	17.19%
$12/64 = 6/32 = 3/16$	0.187 5	18.75%
$13/64$	0.203 125	20.31%
$14/64 = 7/32$	0.218 75	21.88%
$15/64$	0.234 375	23.44%
$16/64 = 8/32 = 4/16 = 2/8 = 1/4$	0.25	25.00%
$17/64$	0.265 625	26.56%
$18/64 = 9/32$	0.281 25	28.13%
$19/64$	0.296 875	29.69%
$20/64 = 10/32 = 5/16$	0.312 5	31.25%
$21/64$	0.328 125	32.81%
$22/64 = 11/32$	0.343 75	34.38%
$23/64$	0.359 375	35.94%
$24/64 = 12/32 = 6/16 = 3/8$	0.375	37.50%

The 64ths table (continued)

Fraction	Decimal	Percentage
$^{25}/_{64}$	0.390 625	39.06%
$^{26}/_{64} = ^{13}/_{32}$	0.406 25	40.63%
$^{27}/_{64}$	0.421 875	42.19%
$^{28}/_{64} = ^{14}/_{32} = ^{7}/_{16}$	0.437 5	43.75%
$^{29}/_{64}$	0.453 125	45.31%
$^{30}/_{64} = ^{15}/_{32}$	0.468 75	46.88%
$^{31}/_{64}$	0.484 375	48.44%
$^{32}/_{64} = ^{16}/_{32} = ^{8}/_{16} = ^{4}/_{8} = ^{2}/_{4} = ^{1}/_{2}$	0.5	50.00%
$^{33}/_{64}$	0.515 625	51.56%
$^{34}/_{64} = ^{17}/_{32}$	0.531 25	53.13%
$^{35}/_{64}$	0.546 875	54.69%
$^{36}/_{64} = ^{18}/_{32} = ^{9}/_{16}$	0.562 5	56.25%
$^{37}/_{64}$	0.578 125	57.81%
$^{38}/_{64} = ^{19}/_{32}$	0.593 75	59.37%
$^{39}/_{64}$	0.609 375	60.94%
$^{40}/_{64} = ^{20}/_{32} = ^{10}/_{16} = ^{5}/_{8}$	0.625	62.50%
$^{41}/_{64}$	0.640 625	64.06%
$^{42}/_{64} = ^{21}/_{32}$	0.656 25	65.63%
$^{43}/_{64}$	0.671 875	67.19%
$^{44}/_{64} = ^{22}/_{32} = ^{11}/_{16}$	0.687 5	68.75%
$^{45}/_{64}$	0.703 125	70.31%
$^{46}/_{64} = ^{23}/_{32}$	0.718 75	71.88%
$^{47}/_{64}$	0.734 375	73.44%
$^{48}/_{64} = ^{24}/_{32} = ^{12}/_{16} = ^{6}/_{8} = ^{3}/_{4}$	0.75	75.00%
$^{49}/_{64}$	0.765 625	76.56%

The 64ths table (continued)

Fraction	Decimal	Percentage
$50/64 = 25/32$	0.781 25	78.13%
$51/64$	0.796 875	79.69%
$52/64 = 26/32 = 13/16$	0.812 5	81.25%
$53/64$	0.828 125	82.81%
$54/64 = 27/32$	0.843 75	84.38%
$55/64$	0.859 375	85.94%
$56/64 = 28/32 = 14/16 = 7/8$	0.875	87.50%
$57/64$	0.890 625	89.06%
$58/64 = 29/32$	0.906 25	90.63%
$59/64$	0.921 875	92.19%
$60/64 = 30/32 = 15/16$	0.937 5	93.75%
$61/64$	0.953 125	95.31%
$62/64 = 31/32$	0.968 75	96.88%
$63/64$	0.984 375	98.44%
$64/64 = 32/32 = 16/16 = 8/8 = 4/4 = 2/2$	1	100.00%

WORKING WITH PERCENTAGES

A percentage means a part of 100, so 20% is the same as $^{20}/_{100}$ and so on. To calculate percentages using a calculator, you sometimes have to convert the fraction (as in $^{20}/_{100}$ or $^1/_5$) into a decimal expression (such as 0.2). With a % key, the calculator will do the 'multiplication by 100' and 'equals' for you. But even when using a calculator, you must know what steps to take.

Calculating percentages: situations

There are three types of situation in which you need to calculate percentages, described below. Many of these occur during sales, when you want to calculate what a percentage discount is equal to from the price of an item. You might also need to calculate the added cost of VAT for something you buy, such as an appliance, that does not have VAT included in its advertised price.

Determining the value of a percentage of a number
● For example: **what is 20% of 600?**

1 Determine the value of 1%:

> 600 is equal to 100%
> 60 is equal to 10%
> so
> 6 is equal to 1%

2 Multiply the value of 1% (in this case 6) by the value you want to determine (in this case 20):

> $6 \times 20 = 120$
> so
> 20% of 600 = 120

● For example: **what is 17½% of £35.00?**

1 Determine the value of 1%:

> 35 is equal to 100%
> 3.5 is equal to 10%
> SO
> 0.35 is equal to 1%

2 Multiply the value of 1% (in this case 0.35) by the value you want to determine (in this case 17.5):

> $0.35 \times 17.5 = 6.125$
> SO
> 17½% of £35.00 = £6.12

Determining what percentage one number is of another number

● For example: **what percentage of 360 is 60?**

1 Divide the smaller number by the larger:

> $60 \div 360 = 0.1666$

2 Convert the result to a percentage by multiplying it by 100:

> $0.1666 \times 100 = 16.66\%$
> SO
> 60 = 16.66% of 360

● For example: **what percentage of 175 is 25?**

As in the example above, do the following calculations:

> $25 \div 175 = 0.1428$
> $0.1428 \times 100 = 14.28\%$
> SO
> 25 = 14.28% of 175

Determining the value of a number when only the value of a percentage of that number is known

● For example: **for what number is 30% equal to 60?**

1 Find the value of 1%:

$$60 \text{ is equal to } 30\%$$
$$\text{so}$$
$$\frac{60}{30} = 2 \text{ is equal to } 1\%$$

2 Multiply the result by 100 to give the number:

$$2 \times 100 = 200$$
$$200 \text{ is equal to } 100\%$$
$$\text{so}$$
$$60 = 30\% \text{ of } 200$$

INTEREST

Interest refers to the charge made for borrowing money or the payment given for investing money. It is usually expressed in terms of percentage rates. There are two types of interest: simple interest and compound interest.

Simple interest

This type of interest is calculated on the amount of money originally loaned (called the principal). The formula used to calculate simple interest is:

$$I = \frac{P \times R \times T}{100}$$

I is interest, P is principal, R is the percentage rate per unit time, and T is the length of time (measured in years) over which the money is invested or loaned. For example, the interest earned when £5000 is invested for 3 years at a rate of 6% per annum (simple interest) is given by:

$$I = \frac{5000 \times 6 \times 3}{100} = £900$$

The final sum – or amount of money to which the principal will grow – is figured using the formula:

$$S \text{ (sum)} = P\left(1 + \frac{R \times T}{100}\right)$$

For example, the sum of money that will be in an
account in which £2800 is invested for 4 years at a rate
of 8% per annum (simple interest) is given by:

$$S = 2800 \left(1 + \frac{8 \times 4}{100}\right) = £3696$$

Compound interest

Unlike simple interest, which is paid only on the
principal, compound interest is paid also on the
previous interest earned. Thus the sum – or amount to
which the principal will grow – increases at a much
faster rate than with simple interest.

Compound interest is figured using the formula:

$$S = P \left(1 + \frac{R}{100}\right)^T$$

For example, the sum of money that will be in an
account in that £2800 is invested for 4 years at a rate of
8% per annum (compound interest) is given by:

$$S = 2800 \times \left(1 + \frac{8}{100}\right)^4 = 2800 \times (1.08)^4 = £3809.37$$

The tables on the following pages show the simple
interest earned on £1000 and £100, and the compound
interest earned on £100 invested at various interest
rates.

Simple interest (in pounds) paid on a principal of £1000

Period	Per cent per annum			
	2.5%	3%	3.5%	4%
1 days	0.01	0.08	0.10	0.11
2 days	0.14	0.16	0.19	0.22
3 days	0.21	0.25	0.29	0.33
4 days	0.27	0.33	0.38	0.44
5 days	0.34	0.41	0.48	0.55
6 days	0.41	0.49	0.58	0.66
30 days	2.06	2.47	2.88	3.29
60 days	4.11	4.93	5.75	6.58
90 days	6.16	7.40	8.63	9.86
180 days	12.33	14.80	17.26	19.73
360 days	24.66	29.59	34.52	39.45
1 year	25.00	30.00	35.00	40.00

 Simple interest (in pounds) added on to a principal of £100

Period	Per cent per annum			
	7%	8%	9%	10%
1 years	107.00	108.00	109.00	110.00
5 years	135.00	140.00	145.00	150.00
10 years	170.00	180.00	190.00	200.00
20 years	240.00	260.00	280.00	300.00
30 years	310.00	340.00	370.00	400.00
40 years	380.00	420.00	460.00	500.00
50 years	450.00	500.00	550.00	600.00

| Per cent per annum | | | | | |
4.5%	5%	5.5%	6%	6.5%	7%
0.12	0.14	0.15	0.16	0.18	0.19
0.25	0.27	0.30	0.39	0.36	0.38
0.37	0.41	0.45	0.49	0.53	0.58
0.49	0.55	0.60	0.66	0.71	0.77
0.62	0.69	0.75	0.82	0.89	0.96
0.74	0.82	0.90	0.99	1.07	1.15
3.70	4.11	4.52	4.93	5.34	5.75
7.40	8.22	9.04	9.86	10.69	11.51
11.10	12.33	13.56	14.80	16.03	17.26
22.19	24.66	27.12	29.59	32.06	34.52
44.38	49.32	54.25	59.18	64.11	69.04
45.00	50.00	55.00	60.00	65.00	70.00

| Per cent per annum | | | | |
11%	12%	13%	14%	15%
111.00	112.00	113.00	114.00	115.00
155.00	160.00	165.00	170.00	175.00
210.00	220.00	230.00	240.00	250.00
320.00	340.00	360.00	380.00	400.00
430.00	460.00	490.00	520.00	550.00
540.00	580.00	620.00	660.00	700.00
650.00	700.00	750.00	800.00	850.00

£ £ Compound interest rates (in pounds) paid on a principal of £100

Period	Per cent per annum			
	4%	5%	6%	7%
1 day	0.01	0.01	0.02	0.02
1 week	0.08	0.10	0.12	0.14
6 months	2.00	2.50	3.00	3.50
1 year	4.00	5.00	6.00	7.00
2 years	8.16	10.25	12.36	14.49
3 years	12.49	15.76	19.10	22.50
4 years	16.99	21.55	26.25	31.08
5 years	21.67	27.63	33.82	40.26
6 years	26.53	34.01	41.85	50.07
7 years	31.59	40.71	50.36	60.58
8 years	36.86	47.75	59.38	71.82
9 years	42.33	55.13	68.95	83.85
10 years	48.02	62.89	79.08	96.72

Comparing simple interest to compound interest

Money grows much more quickly with compound interest than with simple interest. Compare, for example, the amount of time required for an amount of money to double itself with simple interest and with compound interest:

| Per cent per annum | | | | | |
8%	9%	10%	12%	14%	16%
0.02	0.03	0.03	0.03	0.04	0.04
0.15	0.17	0.19	0.23	0.27	0.31
4.00	4.50	5.00	6.00	7.00	8.00
8.00	9.00	10.00	12.00	14.00	16.00
16.64	18.81	21.00	25.44	29.96	34.56
25.97	29.50	33.10	40.49	48.15	56.09
36.05	41.16	46.41	57.35	68.90	81.06
46.93	53.86	61.05	76.23	92.54	110.03
58.69	67.71	77.16	97.38	119.50	143.64
71.38	82.80	94.87	121.07	150.23	182.62
85.09	99.26	114.36	147.60	185.26	227.84
99.90	117.19	135.79	177.31	225.19	280.30
115.89	136.74	159.37	210.58	270.72	341.14

Rate	Simple	Compound
7%	14 yrs, 104 days	10 yrs, 89 days
10%	10 yrs	7 yrs, 100 days

2. In the kitchen

WEIGHING AND MEASURING FOOD AND DRINK

This section introduces metric, imperial and other weights and measures, giving easy conversion tables to help you convert one unit to another (both exact and approximate (or 'handy') measures are given). It contains tables of measures, including spoonfuls, quarts, bushels, etc., and also converts UK and US imperial measures (some are different). You will also find tables of beverage (drink) measures, including alcohol measures.

Weights

Most packaged foods are sold in metric (continental) weights – grams (g) and kilograms (kg). Unpackaged food items are usually sold in imperial (UK) weights – ounces (oz) and pounds (lb). Recipes usually give weights of ingredients in either metric or imperial units. Use the tables on pp. 43–4 to help you convert from metric to imperial and vice versa.

Liquid measures

Most bottled or packaged liquids are sold in metric volumes – litres (l) and millilitres (ml).
Some liquids are sold in imperial volumes – pints (pt) or fluid ounces (fl oz). It is important to remember that UK and US imperial units are not the same. Use the tables on pp. 48–51 to help you convert from metric to UK or US imperial and vice versa.

Other volume measures

With ingredients (especially in American recipes), you
will find other measures are used, mainly spoonfuls and
cups. Some are liquid and some are dry measures. The
number of spoonfuls or cups that make up a given
weight will vary with the density of the ingredient. Use
the tables on p. 56 to help you work out equivalents for
various measures and ingredients.

Beverages

Beverages are also measured in various units, whether
by glass, bottle or barrel. Tables of these units can be
found on pp. 57–9. You will also find tables of alcohol
measures and units.

Measuring ingredients

The rule in most recipes is to use level measures when
using standard measuring cups and spoons.

- For 'dry' ingredients fill the cup or spoon, and level
  it off with a straight-edged knife. If the ingredients
  are lumpy, sift them before you measure them.
- For liquids, always scrape out the cup or spoon to get
  the full measure. A rubber scraper or spatula is a
  useful tool for this.
- Fats are measured more easily at room temperature
  than if cold, when they are hard. Again, make sure
  you get the full measure by scraping out the
  measuring cup or spoon.

WEIGHT

For domestic purposes, the words 'weight' and 'mass' can be taken to mean the same thing.

Imperial units

Imperial units of weight are measured in ounces (oz) and pounds (lb).

$$1 \text{ lb} = 16 \text{ oz}$$
$$\tfrac{1}{2} \text{ lb} = 8 \text{ oz}$$

Note: UK and US imperial weights are the same.

Metric units

Metric units of weight are measured in grams (g) and kilograms (kg).

$$1 \text{ kg} = 1000 \text{ g}$$
$$0.1 \text{ kg} = 100 \text{ g}$$

Imperial to metric conversions

Use the tables opposite for imperial to metric conversions. Here are the main equivalents:

$$1 \text{ lb} = 0.454 \text{ kg or } 454 \text{ g}$$
$$4 \text{ oz} = 113 \text{ g}$$
$$1 \text{ oz} = 28 \text{ g}$$

Metric to imperial conversions

Use the tables on p. 44 for metric to imperial conversions. Here are the main equivalents:

$$1 \text{ kg} = 2.205 \text{ lb or } 35.27 \text{ oz}$$
$$100 \text{ g} = 3.527 \text{ oz}$$
$$10 \text{ g} = 0.353 \text{ oz}$$

Imperial to metric conversion tables

 Ounces and pounds to grams and kilograms

Handy g	Handy kg	oz	Exact g	Exact kg
25	0.025	1	28.35	0.028
50	–	2	56.70	–
75	–	3	85.05	–
100	0.100	4	113.40	0.113
150	–	5	141.75	–
175	–	6	170.10	–
200	–	7	198.45	–
225	0.225	8	226.80	0.227
250	–	9	255.15	–
275	–	10	283.50	–
275	–	11	311.85	–
350	0.350	12	340.20	0.340
375	–	13	368.55	–
400	–	14	396.90	–
425	–	15	425.25	–
450	0.450	16	453.60	0.453

Handy g	Handy kg	lb	Exact g	Exact kg
450	0.45	1	453.60	0.454
900	0.90	2	907.19	0.907
1350	1.35	3	1360.78	1.361
1800	1.80	4	1814.38	1.814
2250	2.25	5	2267.96	2.268
–	2.70	6	–	2.722
–	3.15	7	–	3.175
–	3.60	8	–	3.629
–	4.05	9	–	4.082
–	4.50	10	–	4.536

Metric to imperial conversion tables

Grams and kilograms to ounces and pounds

Handy oz	Handy lb	g	Exact oz	Exact lb
0.35	–	10	0.353	–
0.70	–	20	0.705	–
1.75	–	50	1.764	–
3.50	0.22	100	3.527	0.220
7.00	0.44	200	7.055	0.441
10.50	0.66	300	10.582	0.661
14.00	0.88	400	14.109	0.882
17.50	1.10	500	17.637	1.102
21.00	1.32	600	21.164	1.323
24.50	1.54	700	24.691	1.543
28.00	1.76	800	28.219	1.764
31.50	1.98	900	31.746	1.984
35.00	2.20	1000	35.273	2.205

Handy oz	Handy lb	kg	Exact oz	Exact lb
35.0	2.2	1	35.273	2.205
70.0	4.4	2	70.547	4.409
105.0	6.6	3	105.820	6.614
140.0	8.8	4	141.093	8.818
–	11.0	5	–	11.023
–	13.2	6	–	13.227
–	15.4	7	–	15.432
–	17.6	8	–	17.637
–	19.8	9	–	19.841
–	22.0	10	–	22.046

LIQUID MEASURES

Imperial units (UK)

UK imperial units for liquid measures are measured in fluid ounces (fl oz) and pints (pt).

$$1 \text{ pt} = 20 \text{ fl oz}$$
$$^3/_4 \text{ pt} = 15 \text{ fl oz}$$
$$^1/_2 \text{ pt} = 10 \text{ fl oz}$$
$$^1/_4 \text{ pt} = 5 \text{ fl oz}$$

Imperial units (US)

US imperial units for liquid measures are measured in fluid ounces (US fl oz) and pints (US fl pt).

$$1 \text{ US fl pt} = 16 \text{ US fl oz}$$
$$^3/_4 \text{ US fl pt} = 12 \text{ US fl oz}$$
$$^1/_2 \text{ US fl pt} = 8 \text{ US fl oz}$$
$$^1/_4 \text{ US fl pt} = 4 \text{ US fl oz}$$

Metric units

Metric units for liquid measures are measured in millilitres (ml) and litres (l). Sometimes centilitres (cl) are used.

$$1 \text{ l} = 1000 \text{ ml}$$
$$1 \text{ l} = 100 \text{ cl}$$
$$0.1 \text{ l} = 100 \text{ ml or } 10 \text{ cl}$$
$$1 \text{ cl} = 10 \text{ ml}$$

Imperial (UK) to metric conversions
Use the tables on p. 48 for UK imperial
to metric conversions. Here are the main equivalents:

$$1 \text{ pt} = 568 \text{ ml}$$
$$1/2 \text{ pt} = 284 \text{ ml}$$
$$10 \text{ fl oz} = 284 \text{ ml}$$
$$5 \text{ fl oz} = 142 \text{ ml}$$
$$1 \text{ fl oz} = 28.4 \text{ ml}$$

Metric to imperial (UK) conversions
Use the tables on p. 49 for metric to UK imperial
conversions. Here are the main equivalents:

$$1 \text{ ml} = 0.035 \text{ fl oz}$$
$$10 \text{ ml} = 0.352 \text{ fl oz}$$
$$100 \text{ ml} = 3.52 \text{ fl oz}$$
$$1 \text{ l} = 35.2 \text{ fl oz or } 1.76 \text{ pt}$$

Imperial (US) to metric conversions
Use the tables on p. 50 for US imperial
to metric conversions. Here are the main equivalents:

$$1 \text{ US fl pt} = 473 \text{ ml}$$
$$1/2 \text{ US fl pt} = 237 \text{ cl}$$
$$8 \text{ US fl oz} = 237 \text{ ml}$$
$$4 \text{ US fl oz} = 118 \text{ cl}$$
$$1 \text{ US fl oz} = 29.6 \text{ ml}$$

Metric to imperial (US) conversions
Use the tables on p. 51 for metric to US imperial
conversions. Here are the main equivalents:

$$
\begin{aligned}
1 \text{ ml} &= 0.034 \text{ US fl oz} \\
10 \text{ ml} &= 0.338 \text{ US fl oz} \\
100 \text{ ml} &= 3.381 \text{ US fl oz} \\
1 \text{ l} &= 33.81 \text{ US fl oz or} \\
&\quad 2.113 \text{ US fl pt}
\end{aligned}
$$

Imperial (UK) to imperial (US) conversions
Use the tables on p. 52 for UK imperial to US imperial
conversions. Here are the main equivalents:

$$
\begin{aligned}
1 \text{ pt} &= 1.201 \text{ US fl pt} \\
\tfrac{1}{2} \text{ pt} &= 9.608 \text{ US fl oz} \\
10 \text{ fl oz} &= 9.608 \text{ US fl oz} \\
5 \text{ fl oz} &= 4.804 \text{ US fl oz} \\
1 \text{ fl oz} &= 0.961 \text{ US fl oz}
\end{aligned}
$$

Imperial (US) to imperial (UK) conversions
Use the tables on p. 53 for US imperial to UK imperial
conversions. Here are the main equivalents:

$$
\begin{aligned}
1 \text{ US fl pt} &= 0.833 \text{ pt} \\
\tfrac{1}{2} \text{ US fl pt} &= 8.327 \text{ fl oz} \\
8 \text{ US fl oz} &= 8.327 \text{ fl oz} \\
4 \text{ US fl oz} &= 4.163 \text{ fl oz} \\
1 \text{ US fl oz} &= 1.041 \text{ fl oz}
\end{aligned}
$$

Imperial (UK) to metric conversion tables

 Fluid ounces and pints to millilitres and litres

Handy ml	Handy l	fl oz	Exact ml	Exact l
30	–	1	28.413	–
60	–	2	56.826	–
90	–	3	85.239	–
110	–	4	113.652	–
140	0.15	5	142.065	0.142
170	–	6	170.478	–
200	–	7	198.891	–
230	–	8	227.305	–
260	–	9	255.718	–
280	0.3	10	284.131	0.284
450	0.45	15	426.196	0.426
600	0.6	20	568.261	0.568

Handy fl oz	Handy l	pt	Exact fl oz	Exact l
600	0.6	1	568.261	0.568
1150	1.2	2	1136.522	1.137
1700	1.7	3	1704.783	1.705
2250	2.3	4	2273.044	2.273
–	2.9	5	–	2.841
–	3.4	6	–	3.410
–	4.0	7	–	3.978
–	4.6	8	–	4.546
–	5.1	9	–	5.114
–	5.7	10	–	5.683

Metric to imperial (UK) conversion tables

**Millilitres and litres to
fluid ounces and pints**

Handy fl oz	Handy pt	ml	Exact fl oz	Exact pt
0.35	–	10	0.352	–
0.70	–	20	0.704	–
1.75	–	50	1.760	–
3.50	0.175	100	3.519	0.176
7.00	–	200	7.038	–
10.50	–	300	10.558	–
14.00	–	400	14.076	–
17.50	0.875	500	17.596	0.880
21.00	–	600	21.115	–
24.50	–	700	24.634	–
28.00	–	800	28.154	–
31.50	–	900	31.673	–
35.00	1.75	1000	35.192	1.760

Handy fl oz	Handy pt	l	Exact fl oz	Exact pt
35	1.75	1	35.192	1.760
70	3.50	2	70.384	3.519
105	5.25	3	105.576	5.279
140	7.00	4	140.768	7.039
–	8.75	5	–	8.798
–	10.50	6	–	10.558
–	12.25	7	–	12.317
–	14.00	8	–	14.077
–	15.75	9	–	15.837
–	17.50	10	–	17.596

Imperial (US) to metric conversion tables

 US fluid ounces and US fluid pints to millilitres and litres

Handy ml	Handy l	US fl oz	Exact ml	Exact l
30	–	1	29.574	–
60	–	2	59.147	–
90	–	3	88.721	–
120	0.125	4	118.294	0.118
150	–	5	147.868	–
180	–	6	177.441	–
210	–	7	207.015	–
240	0.250	8	236.588	0.237
270	–	9	266.162	–
300	–	10	295.735	–
360	0.350	12	354.882	0.355
470	0.500	16	473.176	0.473

Handy ml	Handy l	US fl pt	Exact ml	Exact l
480	0.5	1	473.176	0.473
950	0.9	2	946.352	0.946
1420	1.4	3	1419.528	1.420
1900	1.9	4	1892.704	1.893
–	2.4	5	–	2.366
–	2.8	6	–	2.839
–	3.3	7	–	3.312
–	3.8	8	–	3.785
–	4.3	9	–	4.259
–	4.7	10	–	4.732

Metric to imperial (US) conversion tables

 Millilitres and litres to US fluid ounces and US fluid pints

Handy US fl oz	Handy US fl pt	ml	Exact US fl oz	Exact US fl pt
0.35	0.02	10	0.34	0.021
0.70	–	20	0.68	–
1.70	–	50	1.69	–
3.40	0.20	100	3.38	0.211
6.50	–	200	6.76	–
10.00	–	300	10.14	–
13.50	–	400	13.53	–
17.00	1.05	500	16.91	1.057
20.50	–	600	20.29	–
24.00	–	700	23.67	–
27.00	–	800	27.05	–
30.50	–	900	30.43	–
34.00	2.10	1000	33.81	2.113

Handy US fl oz	Handy US fl pt	l	Exact US fl oz	Exact US fl pt
34	2.1	1	33.81	2.113
68	4.2	2	67.63	4.227
101	6.3	3	101.44	6.340
135	8.4	4	135.26	8.454
–	10.5	5	–	10.567
–	12.6	6	–	12.680
–	14.8	7	–	14.794
–	16.9	8	–	16.907
–	19.0	9	–	19.020
–	21.1	10	–	21.134

Imperial (UK) to imperial (US) conversion tables

UK fluid ounces and pints to US fluid ounces and fluid pints

Handy US fl oz	Handy US fl pt	UK fl oz	Exact US fl oz	Exact US fl pt
1.0	–	1	0.961	–
1.9	–	2	1.922	–
2.9	–	3	2.882	–
3.8	–	4	3.843	–
4.8	0.3	5	4.804	0.3
5.8	–	6	5.765	–
6.7	–	7	6.725	–
7.7	–	8	7.686	–
8.6	–	9	8.647	–
9.6	0.6	10	9.608	0.6
10.5	–	11	10.568	–
11.5	0.7	12	11.529	0.721

Handy US fl oz	Handy US fl pt	UK pt	Exact US fl oz	Exact US fl pt
19.2	1.2	1	19.215	1.201
38.4	2.4	2	38.430	2.402
57.6	3.6	3	57.646	3.603
76.9	4.8	4	76.861	4.804
–	6.0	5	–	6.005
–	7.2	6	–	7.206
–	8.4	7	–	8.407
–	9.6	8	–	9.608
–	10.8	9	–	10.809
–	12.0	10	–	12.010

Imperial (US) to imperial (UK) conversion tables

 US fluid ounces and fluid pints to UK fluid ounces and pints

Handy UK fl oz	Handy UK pt	US fl oz	Exact UK fl oz	Exact UK pt
1.0	–	1	1.041	–
2.1	–	2	2.082	–
3.1	–	3	3.122	–
4.2	0.2	4	4.163	0.208
5.2	–	5	5.204	–
6.2	–	6	6.245	–
7.3	–	7	7.286	–
8.3	0.4	8	8.327	0.416
9.4	–	9	9.368	–
10.4	–	10	10.408	–
11.5	–	11	11.449	–
12.5	0.6	12	12.490	0.624

Handy UK fl oz	Handy UK pt	US fl pt	Exact UK fl oz	Exact UK pt
17.0	0.8	1	16.653	0.833
33.5	1.7	2	33.307	1.665
50.0	2.5	3	49.960	2.498
66.5	3.3	4	66.614	3.331
–	4.2	5	–	4.163
–	5.0	6	–	4.996
–	5.8	7	–	5.829
–	6.7	8	–	6.661
–	7.5	9	–	7.494
–	8.3	10	–	8.327

OTHER VOLUME MEASURES
Water weights
The following gives volumes of water and their equivalent weights in UK imperial measures and weights.

```
1 fluid ounce (fl oz) of water = 1 ounce (oz)
           20 fl oz of water = 20 oz or 1¹/₄ pounds (lb)
              pint (pt) of water = 20 oz or 1¹/₄ lb
          quart (qt) of water = 40 oz or 2¹/₂ lb
          gallon (gal) of water = 10 lb (160 oz)
```

Useful US measures
The following are equivalents for other US measures that you may find in recipes.

```
A few grains, a pinch
    or a dash (dry) = less than ¹/₈ teaspoon (tsp)
  A dash (liquid) = a few drops
      1 US minim = ¹/₆₀ US fluid dram (US fl dr) or
                      ¹/₄₈₀ US fl oz
1 US fluid dram = 60 minims
             1 tsp = ¹/₆ US fl oz
1 tablespoon (tbsp) = 3 tsp
      1 US fl oz = 8 US fl dr
            1 gill = 4 US fl oz
            1 cup = 8 US fl oz
       1 US fl pt = 16 US fl oz
       1 US fl pt = 4 gills
```

Useful UK measures

The following are equivalents for other UK measures
that you may find in recipes.

$$1 \text{ minim} = 1 \text{ drop or } \tfrac{1}{60} \text{ dram (dr) or}$$
$$\tfrac{1}{480} \text{ fl oz}$$
$$1 \text{ thimbleful} = 30 \text{ drops or 30 minims}$$
$$1 \text{ dram (dr)} = 60 \text{ drops or 60 minims or}$$
$$1 \text{ tsp}$$
$$1 \text{ dessertspoon} = 2 \text{ dr}$$
$$1 \text{ tbsp} = 4 \text{ dr}$$
$$1 \text{ fl oz} = 8 \text{ dr}$$
$$1 \text{ wine glass} = 2 \text{ fl oz}$$
$$1 \text{ tea cup} = 5 \text{ fl oz}$$
$$1 \text{ gill} = 5 \text{ fl oz or } \tfrac{1}{4} \text{ pt}$$
$$1 \text{ mug} = 10 \text{ fl oz or } \tfrac{1}{2} \text{ pt}$$
$$1 \text{ pt} = 4 \text{ gills}$$
$$1 \text{ pt} = 20 \text{ fl oz}$$

Cups and spoonfuls

The table on the next page gives useful measures and
equivalents for various main cooking ingredients,
including flour, sugar, rice, butter or margarine, and
eggs. These are given in cups, tablespoons or
teaspoons, and converted into ounces (oz) and grams
(g) for weight and fluid ounces (fl oz) and millilitres
(ml) for volume. The cups and spoonfuls used in
American measures are slightly different, as you will
see if you compare the useful UK measures above with
the US ones on the previous page.

Cups and spoonfuls to imperial (UK) and metric
conversion tables

 **Dry ingredients – cups and spoonfuls
to ounces and grams**

Ingredients	Cups/spoonfuls	oz	g
Bread crumbs	1 cup	7	200
Brown sugar	1 cup	6	170
White sugar	1 cup	8	225
	1 tablespoon	1	25
Flour	1 cup	5	140
	1 tablespoon	$^3/_4$	20
Currants	1 cup	5	140
Sultanas	1 cup	7	200
Rice (uncooked)	1 cup	7	200
Butter or margarine	1 cup	8	225

 **Wet ingredients – cups and spoonfuls
to fluid ounces and millilitres**

Ingredients	Cups/spoonfuls	fl oz	ml
1 egg	2$^1/_2$ tablespoons*	1$^1/_4$	35
$^1/_2$ egg	4 teaspoons*	$^2/_3$	18
1 egg white	2 tablespoons*	1	28
1 egg yolk	1 tablespoon*	$^1/_2$	15
4–6 egg whites	$^1/_2$ cup	4	112
6–7 egg yolks	$^1/_2$ cup	4	112
Water, milk or other liquid	1 tablespoon (*approx)	$^1/_2$	15

BEVERAGES
Standard contents per bottle – wine, sherry and spirits

The number of glasses in a bottle is usually based on the following pub measures:

1 wine glass = 114 millilitres (ml) or
4 fluid ounces (fl oz)
1 sherry glass = 50 ml or 1/3 gill
1 spirit measure = 25 ml or 1/6 gill
(England/Wales)
1 spirit measure = 30 ml or 1/5 gill (Scotland)

Standard bottle contents

Bottle		cl/ml	Glass/measure	
	Wine	75 cl 750 ml		6 1/2 glasses
	Sherry	75 cl 750 ml		15 glasses
	Spirits	70 cl 700 ml		28 measures (England/Wales)
				23 1/2 measures (Scotland)

Alcoholic units per glass – beer, spirits and wines
The table below is a rough guide for comparing the
strengths of different alcoholic drinks. The unit system
is a rough guide because alcoholic percentages of
drinks can vary (for example, some brands and types of
beer are stronger than others), so affecting the units of
alcohol per measure. One standard unit is equivalent to
8 grams (g) of alcohol.

**Alcoholic units per
standard measure**

Drink	Glass/measure	Units of alcohol
Beer: lager cider	1 pt	2
Spirits: vodka rum whisky gin, etc.	single measure 25 ml/¹⁄₆ gill	1
Wine	standard glass 114 ml/4 fl oz	1
Fortified wine: sherry madeira port, etc.	small glass 50 ml/¹⁄₃ gill	1

Alcoholic content per bottle – beer, spirits and wines

Alcoholic content is given as a percentage of a beverage. It can vary in beverages of similar type and volume. One 750 ml bottle of wine may have an alcoholic content of 7% while another has 13%. Alcoholic content can also be expressed as units.

 Alcoholic content and units per bottle

Drink	Bottle size	% alcohol per bottle	Units per bottle
Beer: low alcohol	(any)	0.05	1/25
		0.5	1/2
		1	1
Beer and wine	75 cl/750 ml	3	2
		5	4
		6	4 1/2
Wine	75 cl/750 ml	7	5 1/2
		9	7
		11	8
		13	10
Fortified wine	75 cl/750 ml	15	11 1/2
		17	13
		20	15
		23	17 1/2
		25	19
		27	20
Spirits	70 cl/700 ml	37	26
		40	28
		43	30

Beverage measures

Over the years, beverages have been measured by various systems. The following tables are units of measure by glass and US spirit measures, and for beer and wine.

Glass measures

The following is a table of drinks glasses with their equivalent volume in UK imperial units.

$$
\begin{array}{rcl}
\text{1 small jigger} & = & \text{1 fl oz} \\
\text{1 small wine glass} & = & \text{2 fl oz} \\
\text{1 cocktail glass} & = & \text{4 fl oz} \\
\text{1 large sherry glass} & = & \text{4 fl oz} \\
\text{1 large wine glass} & = & \text{4 fl oz} \\
\text{1 tumbler} & = & \text{8 fl oz}
\end{array}
$$

US spirit measures

The following are US spirit measures and their US imperial equivalents.

$$
\begin{array}{rcl}
\text{1 pony} & = & \text{1/2 jigger} \\
\text{1 shot} & = & \text{1 US fl oz} \\
\text{1 shot} & = & \text{2/3 jiggers} \\
\text{1 jigger} & = & \text{1}\tfrac{1}{2}\text{ shots} \\
\text{1 US fl pt} & = & \text{16 shots} \\
\text{1 fifth} & = & \text{25.6 shots or 1.6 US fl pt} \\
\text{1 US fl qt} & = & \text{32 shots or 1}\tfrac{1}{4}\text{ fifths}
\end{array}
$$

Beer measures

The following is a table of beer measures with their equivalents in UK imperial units.

1 small = $\frac{1}{2}$ pt
1 pt = 1 large
1 qt = 2 pt
1 flagon = 1 qt
1 gallon (gal) = 4 qt
1 firkin = 9 gal
1 anker = 10 gal
1 kilderkin = 2 firkins
1 barrel = 2 kilderkins
1 hogshead = $1\frac{1}{2}$ barrels
1 butt = 2 hogsheads
1 tun = 2 butts or 216 gal

Wine measures

The following is a table of wine barrel measures with equivalents in UK imperial units.

1 anker = 10 gal
1 hogshead = 63 gal
1 pipe = 2 hogsheads
1 tun = 2 pipes or 252 gal
1 puncheon = 84 gal
1 butt (sherry) = 110 gal

BUYING FOOD AND DRINK

When buying food there are many factors such as individual preference, nutritional requirement, cost, availability, storage, cooking facilities and so on to consider. Nowadays, most fruits and vegetables are available all year round. Buying fruit and vegetables that are 'in season', however, helps guarantee good quality at low prices.

When to buy fruit

When to buy vegetables

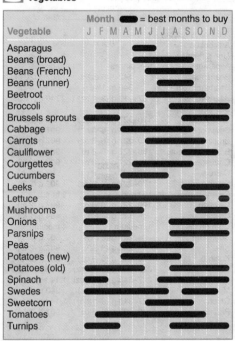

	Month		= best months to buy
Vegetable	J F M A M J J A S O N D		

**Vegetables to buy
for one or four people**

Type	1 person	4 people
Artichokes (globe)	1	4
Artichokes (Jerusalem)	1	4
Asparagus	6–8 pieces	30 pieces
Beans (baked)	142 g (5 oz)	567 g (20 oz)
Beans (broad)	340 g (12 oz)	1.4 kg (3 lb)
Beans (dried)	57–113 g (2–4 oz)	340 g (12 oz)
Beans (French or runner)	170–227 g (6–8 oz)	907 g (2 lb)
Beetroot	170–227 g (6–8 oz)	907 g (2 lb)
Broccoli	170–227 g (6–8 oz)	907 g (2 lb)
Brussels sprouts	170–227 g (6–8 oz)	907 g (2 lb)
Cabbage	170–227 g (6–8 oz)	907 g (2 lb)
Carrots	170–227 g (6–8 oz)	907 g (2 lb)
Cauliflower	170–227 g (6–8 oz)	907 g (2 lb)
Celery	1/2 head	2 heads
Celeriac	170–227 g (6–8 oz)	907 g (2 lb)
Chicory	113 g (4 oz)	454 g (1 lb)
Corn on the cob	1 medium	4 medium
Courgette	227 g (8 oz)	907 g (2 lb)
Kale	227 g (8 oz)	907 g (2 lb)
Kohlrabi	170–227 g (6–8 oz)	907 g (2 lb)
Leeks	227–340 g (8–12 oz)	1.14 kg (2 1/2 lb)
Marrow	227–340 g (8–12 oz)	1.14 kg (2 1/2 lb)
Mushrooms	57–113 g (2–4 oz)	340 g (12 oz)
Onion	227–340 g (8–12 oz)	1.14 kg (2 1/2 lb)
Parsnips	170–227 g (6–8 oz)	907 g (2 lb)

continued

Vegetables to buy (continued)

Type	1 person	4 people
Peas	227 g (8 oz)	907 g (2 lb)
Peas (dried)	227 g (8 oz)	907 g (2 lb)
Potatoes (baked)	1 medium	4 medium
Potatoes (boiled)	170–227 g (6–8 oz)	907 g (2 lb)
Potatoes (chips)	170 g (6 oz)	680 g (1½ lb)
Potatoes (roast)	113–170 g (4–6 oz)	680 g (1½ lb)
Spinach	227 g (8 oz)	907 g (2 lb)
Swedes	170–227 g (6–8 oz)	907 g (2 lb)
Turnips	170–227 g (6–8 oz)	907 g (2 lb)
Tomatoes	113–170 g (4–6 oz)	680 g (1½ lb)
Watercress	30–57 g (1–2 oz)	170 g (6 oz)

 Seafood to buy for one or four people

Type	1 person	4 people
Crab	1 small	4 small/2 large
Cutlets	227 g (8 oz)	907 g (2 lb)
Fillets	170–227 g (6–8 oz)	907 g (2 lb)
Fish (whole)	227–340 g (8–12 oz)	907 g–1.4 kg (2–3 lb)
Lobster	227–340 g (8–12 oz)	907 g–1.4 kg (2–3 lb)
Mussels	568 ml (1pt)	2.27 l (4 pt)
Prawns	284 ml (½ pt)	1.14 l (2 pt)

**Meats to buy
for one or four people**

Type	1 person	4 people
Cooked	85–113 g (3–4 oz)	454 g (1 lb)
With bone	227–340 g (8–12 oz)	907 g–1.4 kg (2–3 lb)
Without bone	113–170 g (4–6 oz)	680 g (1½ lb)
Bacon	2 rashers	8 rashers
Beef stew	284 g (10 oz)	1.14 kg (2½ lb)
Pâté	30 g (1 oz)	113 g (4 oz)
Salami	57 g (2 oz)	227 g (8 oz)
Sausage	113 g (4 oz)	454 g (1 lb)
Shepherd's pie	284 g (10 oz)	1.14 kg (2½ lb)
Steak and kidney pie	227 g (8 oz)	907 g (2 lb)

 **Miscellaneous foods to buy
for one or four people**

Type	1 person	4 people
Canned fruits	113 g (4 oz)	454 g (1 lb)
Cheese	30–57 g (1-2 oz)	170 g (6 oz)
Custard	142 g (5 oz)	568 g (1¼ lb)
Gravy	70 ml (2½ fl oz)	284 ml (½ pt)
Macaroni	113 g (4 oz)	454 g (1 lb)
Nuts	30–57 g (1-2 oz)	170 g (6 oz)
Porridge	30 g (1 oz)	113 g (4 oz)
Pulses	113 g (4 oz)	454 g (1 lb)
Rice	57 g (2 oz)	227 g (8 oz)
Soup	284 ml (½ pt)	1.14 l (2 pt)
Spaghetti	113 g (4 oz)	454 g (1 lb)
Trifle	170 g (6 oz)	680 g (1½ lb)

Buying food for parties

Here are some easy-to-remember servings of particular foods for parties, small and large.

 Small parties of up to six people

Food	Serving
Bridge rolls	85–113 g (3–4 oz)
Cakes (small)	2 per person
Cakes (fruit)	an 18 cm (7 in) cake gives 8 portions
Cakes (wedding)	57 g (2 oz) per person
Chicken	1 large chicken serves 6–7
Cream	284 ml ($1/2$ pt) serves 6 portions
Fruit salad	568 ml (1 pt) serves 6 people
Ice cream	568 ml (1 pt) serves 6 people
Jelly	568 ml (1 pt) serves 6 people
Sandwiches	4 halves per person
Sausage rolls	2 each

 Large parties of up to 100 people

Food	Quantity
Butter	57 g (2 lb)
Coffee	1.14 kg ($2^1/2$ lb)
Cream (whipped)	2.25 l (2 qt)
Ice cream	14 l (3 gal)
Peas	11 kg (25 lb)
Potatoes	16 kg (35 lb)
Roast beef	18 kg (40 lb)
Roast chicken	27 kg (60 lb)
Roast pork	16 kg (36 lb)
Tea	227 g ($1/2$ lb)

Buying drink for parties, receptions and weddings
When buying drink, consider the stages of a celebration.
Estimate how much each guest might be expected to
drink at each stage. The table below offers a guide for

 **Buying drink
for parties**

Occasion	Drink	Allowance per person
Arrival at wedding reception	Sherry	2 glasses
	Champagne or sparkling wine	2 glasses
During a meal	Wine (red/white/rosé)	3–4 glasses
	Champagne or sparkling wine	3 glasses
Toasts	Champagne	1 glass
After-dinner drinks	Whisky, brandy gin	3–4 glasses
	Liqueurs	2–3 glasses
	Squash (average bottle)	3–4 glasses
	Mixers Tonic/soda/juices	

the number of bottles needed for various drinks. Adjust the figures for guests who tend to drink more or less than average, are teetotal or are likely to be driving and not drinking.

Bottle size	Glasses per bottle	Bottles per 20 guests
75 cl (750 ml)	10–15 (²/₃ full)	4
75 cl (750 ml)	6–8 (almost full)	6–8
75 cl (750 ml)	6–8 (²/₃ full)	8–10
75 cl (750 ml)	6–8 (almost full)	8–10
75 cl (750 ml)	6–8 (almost full)	3
70 cl (700 ml)	28 (bar measures)	2
70 cl (700 ml)	28 (bar measures)	1–2
1 litre	18 (medium/long drinks)	4
25 cl (250 ml)	1 (long mixer) or 2 (short ones)	40–80

COOKING WITH GAS AND ELECTRIC OVENS

Oven temperatures

On electric cookers, oven temperatures are given in Celsius (°C) or Fahrenheit (°F). On gas cookers, the oven temperature is shown in gas marks (regulo).

Oven temperatures in Celsius, Fahrenheit and gas mark

Oven heat	°C	°F	Gas mark
Very cool	110	225	1/4
	120	250	1/2
Cool	140	275	1
	150	300	2
Warm	160	325	3
Moderate	180	350	4
Fairly hot	190	375	5
	200	400	6
Hot	220	425	7
	230	450	8
Very hot	240	475	9

Note: Cooking times vary depending on the type of oven used and the condition of the food. The cooking times provided on the following pages are for general guidance only. You must also allow for the oven to reach its operating temperature; the time this requires will vary according to the type of oven used. Always refer to the oven instruction manual and follow the manufacturer's advice. Also, check the food periodically to see if it's ready.

Cooking times for fresh vegetables

Vegetables keep more of their nutritional value when
cooked in a minimum amount of water and not for too
long. Here are recommended times (in minutes) for
steaming (the more nutritious cooking method) and
boiling (N/R means boiling is not recommended).

 **Vegetable cooking times
for steaming and boiling**

Vegetable	Steaming	Boiling
Artichoke, Jerusalem (whole)	15–40	15–40
Asparagus (spears)	12–16	10–15
Beans, broad (shelled)	8–12	7–10
Beans, French (whole)	10–14	8–12
Beans, runner (cut)	8–12	7–10
Broccoli	15–20	8–12
Brussels sprouts (whole)	8–14	6–12
Cabbage, green (shredded)	8–12	5–8
Carrots (sliced)	10–15	8–10
Cauliflower (florets)	10–15	8–10
Celery (sliced)	20–25	15–18
Courgettes	5–10	4–6
Leeks (whole)	15–20	10–15
Mangetout (whole)	5–8	4–6
Marrow/squash (diced)	10–20	N/R
Onions (whole)	30–40	20–30
Parsnips (quartered if large)	30–40	20–30
Peas (shelled)	10–20	6–8
Potatoes (quartered if large)	20–35	15–30
Pumpkin (diced)	20–30	N/R
Spinach	5–12	N/R
Swedes and turnips (sliced)	20–30	15–20
Sweetcorn (cobs)	10–15	6–12

Soaking pulses
- Use plenty of slightly salted water. Pulses absorb water and will swell up to between two and three times their original bulk.
- Here is a quick method of preparing pulses that is equivalent to an overnight (8–12-hour) soak. Bring the pulses to the boil, simmer for 3–5 minutes, and then leave to stand in the water for an hour.

●● Pulses – soaking and
●● cooking time

Pulse	Soaking (hours)	Boiling (minutes)	Special precautions
Lentils (whole)	–	30–45	–
Lentils (split)	–	15–30	–
Chick peas	8–12	60–90	Yes*
Split peas	–	40–45	–
Large beans (broad, butter, pinto)	8–12	50–90	Yes*
Small beans (aduki, black-eyed, mung, red kidney)	8–12	45–50	Yes*
Soya beans	8–12	120–150	Yes•

Special precautions
* Boil uncovered for the first 10 minutes to destroy toxins in skin.
• Boil hard for the first 60 minutes

Meat roasting times and oven settings

Meat	Oven setting	Roasting time
Beef and lamb	*For fast roast:* 30 mins at 220 °C (gas mark 7), then at 200 °C (gas mark 6)	*Thin joints:* 15 mins per 454 g (1 lb) plus 15 mins *Thick joints:* 20–25 mins per 454 g (1 lb) plus 20–25 mins
	For slow roast: 190 °C (gas mark 5)	*Thin joints:* 20 mins per 454 g (1 lb) plus 20 mins *Thick joints:* 33 mins per 454 g (1 lb) plus 33 mins
Veal and pork	*For fast roast:* 30 mins at 220 °C (gas mark 7) then at 200 °C (gas mark 6)	30 mins per 454 g (1 lb) plus 30 mins
	For slow roast: 190 °C (gas mark 5)	35 mins per 454 g (1 lb) plus 35 mins

⚫⚫ Poultry roasting times
⚫⚫ and oven settings

Poultry	Oven settings	Roasting time
Chicken	200 ºC (gas mark 6)	20 mins per 454 g (1 lb) plus 20 mins
Duck	190 ºC (gas mark 5)	20 mins per 454 g (1 lb)
Goose	*For fast roast:* 200 ºC (gas mark 6)	15 mins per 454 g (1 lb) plus 15 mins
	For slow roast: 180 ºC (gas mark 4)	25–30 mins per 454 g (1 lb)
Turkey (stuffed)	*For fast roast:* 230 ºC (gas mark 8)	2$\frac{1}{2}$–3 hrs for 2.7–5.4 kg (6–12 lb) bird; 3–3$\frac{1}{2}$ hrs for 5.4–8.2 kg (12–18 lb) bird
	For slow roast: 170 ºC (gas mark 3)	3$\frac{1}{2}$–4 hrs for 2.7–5.4 kg (6–12 lb) bird; 4–4$\frac{3}{4}$ hrs for 5.4–8.2 kg (12–18 lb) bird

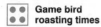

Game bird roasting times

Bird	Cooking time at 220–230 °C (gas mark 7–8) for an average-sized bird (mins)
Grouse	30
Partridge	30
Pheasant	45–60
Pigeon	30
Plover	20–30
Quail	20–30
Snipe	20–30
Wild duck	30
Woodcock	20–30

Hints and tips on roasting meat

Most meats, particularly dry meats such as veal and game, become tough and dry if they are roasted unprotected. A few tips on how to prevent this are given below.

- Put animal or vegetable fat on the meat. This will melt and moisten the meat as it cooks.
- Wrap the meat in cooking foil or a roasting bag to retain its juices. Brown the meat unwrapped at the beginning or end of cooking.
- Alternatively, the meat can be cooked unwrapped but basted regularly.

Note: Duck and goose should be roasted unprotected on an oven rack or trivet to allow the fat to drain away.

COOKING WITH A MICROWAVE OVEN

In microwave ovens, microwaves are directed into the chamber where the food is placed. The microwaves pass through the food and agitate the water molecules in it. The friction produced by the moving water molecules generates heat which is conducted through the food.

Power settings

Microwave ovens have different power level settings for different uses – cooking food, reheating cold food or defrosting frozen food. These settings are shown in the table opposite. In most microwave ovens, the highest power setting is 10 and the lower settings are numbered 1–9.

The role of the timer In most microwave ovens, the oven always operates on full power, but a timer switches the microwave supply on and off according to the setting. For example, adjusting the setting to 5 means that the power output is still 700 W (full power) but the supply is only operating for half the time. If the timer is set for 5 minutes, the microwave supply will be switched on for 30 seconds and then off for 30 seconds throughout the cycle, so that the supply will be on for only 2 minutes 30 seconds in every 5 minutes.

The setting and power control In technically advanced microwave ovens, the power output of the cooker is controlled by the setting. For example, adjusting the setting to 5 reduces the power output from 700 W (full power) to 350 W (half power).

Microwave oven power settings and uses

Power setting	Use
10 or full/high	For cooking vegetables, poultry, fish and some sauces. For starting off joints of meat.
8 or roast	For cooking or reheating joints of meat.
6–7 or medium	For cooking chops and chicken pieces and baking cakes.
4–5 or simmer	For slow-cooking casseroles, for cooking egg and cheese dishes and defrosting large joints.
3 or defrost	Generally for defrosting. For melting chocolate and for delicate sauces.
2 or very low	For softening butter and cream cheese from the refrigerator. For keeping cooked food warm.

Microwave oven timings

The time taken for food to cook inside a microwave oven depends on:

- the nature of the food (for example, 1 lb of potatoes takes less time to cook than 1 lb of cauliflower);
- the power of the oven (a 700 W oven is more powerful than a 600 W oven and will cook food more quickly);
- the power setting used (food will cook more quickly at a setting of 10 than a setting of 5); and
- the quantity of food being cooked (2 lb of potatoes will take more time to cook than 1 lb of potatoes).

Most recipe books give microwave cooking times based on a 700 W microwave oven. Use the tables on the following pages to convert the cooking times of different power outputs. For example, an item that takes 10 minutes to cook in a 700 W oven will take 14 minutes to cook in a 600 W oven.

> *Note:* Cooking times vary, as explained above. The microwave cooking times provided on the following pages are for general guidance only. Always refer to your microwave instruction manual and follow the manufacturer's advice.

Microwave oven timings

Cooking times at different power outputs (wattage)

Wattage	Cooking time (minutes)										
700	5	10	15	20	25	30	40	50	60
650	6	12	17	23	29	35	46	58	69
600	7	14	20	27	33	40	53	67	80
500	8	17	25	33	41	50	66	83	100

Note: Most foods require a standing time of at least 3–5 minutes after being microwaved and before being eaten.

Cooking times in minutes for different quantities of food

The first column shows cooking times for both meat and vegetables. In the other columns, vegetable cooking times are on the left and meat cooking times are on the right.

1 portion (vegetables and meat)	2 portions (vegetables • meat)	4 portions (vegetables • meat)	6 portions (vegetables • meat)
5	7 • 8	10 • 13	15 • 20
10	14 • 16	20 • 25	30 • 40
15	21 • 24	30 • 38	45 • 60
20	28 • 32	40 • 50	60 • 80
25	35 • 40	50 • 63	75 • 100
30	42 • 48	60 • 75	90 • 120
40	56 • 64	80 • 100	120 • 160
50	70 • 80	100 • 125	150 • 200
60	84 • 96	120 • 150	180 • 240

Note: These values are a rough guide.

STORING AND PRESERVING FOOD

In a larder or food cupboard

Such spaces should maintain a temperature of 10 °C (50 °F) or below and be ventilated. When storing food, be guided by the 'best before' or 'use by' date on the product or refer to the table below.

Food storage times in larder or food cupboard

Food	Storage time
Canned fish and meats (except ham)	5 years
Canned fizzy drinks	6–12 months
Canned fruit and juices (except rhubarb and prunes)	1 year
Canned meals, soups and vegetables	2 years
Canned milk	6–12 months
Cake or pastry mixes	6 months
Dried fruit	2–3 months
Dried peas, beans and lentils	6–12 months
Dried yeast	6 months
Flour	6 months
Instant potato	9 months
Jams and marmalade	1 year
Loose tea and coffee	1 month
Milk powder	3 months
Packet soups	1 year
Pasta and rice	1 year
Sugar	5 years

In a refrigerator

A refrigerator's main compartment works by keeping food at between 0 and 5 °C (32 and 41 °F). At this temperature, the activity of food-spoiling microbes (and therefore food decay) is slowed down but not stopped.

 Food storage times in the main compartment of a fridge

Food	Storage time
Butter	2–3 weeks
Margarine	2–3 months
Hard cheese	1–2 weeks
Soft cheese	3–4 weeks
Cooking fat	12 months
Eggs	3–4 weeks
Fish (uncooked)	1 day
Shellfish (uncooked)	1 day
Green vegetables	5–7 days
Green salads	5–7 days
Red meat (uncooked)	2–3 days
Cold meats	5–7 days
Canned ham	6 months
Poultry (uncooked)	2 days
Milk	3–4 days
Yogurt	7–14 days

Freezing

A freezer works by keeping food at −18 °C (0 °F). At this temperature, food-spoiling microbes are inactive and the natural food-spoiling chemicals in food (enzymes) are deactivated. Buying produce in bulk and then freezing it is an effective way to save money.

Tips for home freezing

- Keep the freezer filled with food – this lowers running costs.
- Freeze only fresh food that is in good condition.
- Pack food in small quantities.
- Wrap the food in a polythene freezer bag.
- Wrap food tightly and exclude air to prevent 'freezer burn'.
- Label the packages with the contents and date frozen.
- Introduce no more than one tenth of the freezer's capacity in a day.
- Don't put warm foods in the freezer as it creates condensation.
- When freezing liquids leave 1 cm (1/2 in) of space at the top of the container to allow for expansion.

Frozen foods (not fruit and vegetables): storage times and thawing instructions

Food	Maximum storage time	Special thawing instructions
Fresh bread	4 weeks	Thaw in wrapping
Cakes and pastry	4 weeks	Thaw in wrapping
Casseroles	1 month	Cook from frozen
Sauces, soups and stock	1 month	Heat gently from frozen
Fish (raw)	4 months	Thaw in wrapping
Shellfish (raw)	1 month	Thaw in wrapping
Beef	10 months	Thaw in wrapping in refrigerator, allowing 5 hrs per lb (500 g)
Lamb	8 months	
Pork	4 months	
Ham and bacon (unsliced)	3 months	
Poultry (4–5 lb)	9 months	Thaw overnight in refrigerator
Turkey (9–10 lb)	9 months	Thaw for 36 hrs in refrigerator

Note: Some foods – shellfish and poultry, for example – need to be defrosted thoroughly before cooking.

Frozen fruit and vegetables: preparation instructions and storage times

Food	Preparation instructions	Maximum storage time (months)
Asparagus	Blanch for 3–4 mins	12
Beans (French)	Blanch for 2–3 mins	12
Beans (runner)	Blanch for 2 mins	6
Beetroot	Cook and skin	6
Broccoli	Blanch for 3–4 mins	12
Brussels sprouts	Blanch for 4–6 mins	12
Carrots (scraped)	Blanch for 5–6 mins	12
Cauliflower	Blanch for 3–4 mins	6
Celery	Blanch for 3 mins	12
Courgettes (small)	Blanch for 1 min	12
Leeks (sliced)	Blanch for 1–3 mins	12
Mushrooms	Freeze unblanched	1
Onions (sliced)	Freeze unblanched	3
Peas	Blanch for 1–2 mins	12
Potatoes (chips)	Blanch in oil for 4 mins	6
Potatoes (boiled)	Freeze from cold	6
Spinach	Blanch for 1 min	12
Sweetcorn (cob)	Blanch for 6–10 mins	9
Tomatoes	Freeze unblanched	12

Blanching involves placing the food in boiling water for a short time. The food is then rinsed in cold water. Blanching destroys food-spoiling chemicals and helps seal the surface to keep in the nutrients and retain colour.

FOOD CALORIE CONTENT FINDER
The tables that follow provide a guide to the calorie content found in 30 g (1 oz) of certain foods and drinks.

Fruit (fresh, unless stated)

Fruit	Calories per 30 g (1 oz)	Size of average portion	Calories per portion
Apple	10	1 medium	60
Avocado pear	65	½ large	250
Banana	15	1 medium	75
Cherries	10	113 g (4 oz)	45
Fruit salad (canned)	25	113 g (4 oz)	110
Grapefruit	3	½ medium	15
Grapes	20	113 g (4 oz)	70
Melon (honeydew)	4	1 medium slice	25
Melon (water)	5	1 large slice	50
Orange	5	1 large	40
Peaches	10	1 large	35
Peaches (canned)	25	113 g (4 oz)	100
Pear (raw)	10	1 small	45
Pear (canned)	20	113 g (4 oz)	90
Pineapple	15	113 g (4 oz)	55
Pineapple (canned)	20	113 g (4 oz)	90
Plums	10	1 medium	10

continued

Fruit (continued)

Fruit	Calories per 30 g (1 oz)	Size of average portion	Calories per portion
Prunes (dried)	40	30 g (1 oz)	40
Prunes (canned)	25	113 g (4 oz)	100
Raisins (dried)	70	30 g (1 oz)	70
Raspberries	5	113 g (4 oz)	25
Raspberries (canned)	25	113 g (4 oz)	100
Rhubarb (canned or stewed)	15	142 g (5 oz)	75
Strawberries	10	170 g (6 oz)	45
Strawberries (canned)	25	142 g (5 oz)	125

Cal Dairy products (other than cheese)

Dairy product	Calories per 30 g (1 oz)	Size of average portion	Calories per portion
Butter	210	1 pat	50
Cream (single)	60	small carton	240
Soured cream	55	30 ml (1 fl oz)	55
Milk (whole)	20	30 ml (1 fl oz)	20
Milk (semi-skimmed)	15	30 ml (1 fl oz)	15
Milk (skimmed)	10	30 ml (1 fl oz)	10
Yogurt (natural)	15	small carton	75
Yogurt (fruit)	30	small carton	135

Cal Vegetables (boiled or steamed, unless stated)

Vegetable	Calories per 30 g (1 oz)	Size of average portion	Calories per portion
Aubergine (fried)	60	113 g (4 oz)	240
Beans (baked)	20	142 g (5 oz)	100
Beans (French)	2	142 g (5 oz)	10
Broccoli	5	113 g (4 oz)	20
Brussels sprouts	5	170 g (6 oz)	30
Cabbage	4	113 g (4 oz)	15
Carrots	5	113 g (4 oz)	20
Cauliflower	3	113 g (4 oz)	10
Celery	2	57 g (2 oz)	5
Corn on the cob	35	1 medium	175
Leek	5	113 g (4 oz)	20
Mushrooms (fried)	60	57 g (2 oz)	120
Onions (fried)	100	30 g (1 oz)	100
Parsnips	15	113 g (4 oz)	60
Peas	15	85 g (3 oz)	45
Peppers	4	57 g (2 oz)	10
Potatoes (baked)	30	1 small	120
Potatoes (boiled)	25	113 g (4 oz)	100
Potatoes (chips)	70	170 g (6 oz)	430
Potatoes (crisps)	150	1 small packet	125
Potatoes (roast)	45	2 small	180
Spinach	10	170 g (6 oz)	50
Swede	5	170 g (6 oz)	30
Tomatoes (fried)	20	1 medium	80
Turnip	4	170 g (6 oz)	25

Cal Drinks

Drink	Calories per 30 ml (1 fl oz)	Size of average portion	Calories per portion
Beer	10	284 ml (1/2 pt)	100
Wine (red)	20	142 ml (1/4 pt)	100
Wine (white)	20	142 ml (1/4 pt)	100
Apple juice	15	142 ml (1/4 pt)	65
Cola (nondiet)	10	284 ml (1/2 pt)	110
Coffee (instant)	30	1 teaspoon	2
Drinking chocolate	105	2 teaspoons	35
Grape juice	20	142 ml (1/4 pt)	100
Orange juice	10	142 ml (1/4 pt)	50
Pineapple juice	15	142 ml (1/4 pt)	75
Lemonade	5	284 ml (1/2 pt)	60
Milk (whole)	20	30 ml (1 fl oz)	20
Milk (semi-skimmed)	15	30 ml (1 fl oz)	15
Milk (skimmed)	10	30 ml (1 fl oz)	10
Tea	15	1 teaspoon	1
Tomato juice	4	142 ml (1/4 pt)	20

Cal Meat

Meat	Calories per 30 g (1 oz)	Size of average portion	Calories per portion
Bacon (fried)	135	2 rashers	270
Bacon (grilled)	120	2 rashers	190
Beef (roast)	100	113 g (4 oz)	400
Beef steak (fried)	65	170 g (6 oz)	390
Beef steak (grilled)	55	170 g (6 oz)	330
Beef stew	35	284 g (10 oz)	350
Beefburger	75	1 average	300
Chicken (boiled)	50	142 g (5 oz)	255
Chicken (roast)	60	142 g (5 oz)	290
Gammon (boiled)	75	113 g (4 oz)	300
Goose (roast)	90	113 g (4 oz)	360
Ham (boiled)	75	85 g (3 oz)	230
Ham (smoked)	60	85 g (3 oz)	190
Lamb chop (grilled)	100	113 g (4 oz)	400
Lamb (roast)	80	113 g (4 oz)	320
Liver (lamb, fried)	65	113 g (4 oz)	260
Pork chop (grilled)	95	170 g (6 oz)	565
Pork pie	105	113 g (4 oz)	420
Pâté (various)	95	30 g (1 oz)	95
Salami	140	57 g (2 oz)	280

continued

Meat (continued)

Meat	Calories per 30 g (1 oz)	Size of average portion	Calories per portion
Sausage (pork, fried)	90	2 sausages	360
Sausage (pork, grilled)	90	2 sausages	250
Shepherd's pie	35	284 g (10 oz)	350
Steak and kidney pie	80	227 g (8 oz)	640
Turkey (roast)	50	113 g (4 oz)	200
Veal (roast)	65	113 g (4 oz)	260

Cal Cheeses

Cheese	Calories per 30 g (1 oz)	Size of average portion	Calories per portion
Cheddar	120	30 g (1 oz)	120
Cheshire cheese	120	30 g (1 oz)	120
Cottage cheese	25	small carton	100
Cream cheese	125	30 g (1 oz)	125
Danish Blue	100	30 g (1 oz)	100
Edam	85	30 g (1 oz)	85
Gouda	85	30 g (1 oz)	85
Red Leicester	110	30 g (1 oz)	110
Stilton	130	30 g (1 oz)	130
Wensleydale	110	30 g (1 oz)	110

Cal Fish and shellfish

Fish or shellfish	Calories per 30 g (1 oz)	Size of average portion	Calories per portion
Cod (fried in batter)	55	170 g (6 oz)	340
Crab (boiled)	35	113 g (4 oz)	140
Haddock (fried in breadcrumbs)	50	142 g (5 oz)	250
Herring (fried in oatmeal)	65	142 g (5 oz)	330
Kipper (steamed)	60	142 g (5 oz)	290
Lobster (boiled)	35	142 g (5 oz)	175
Mackerel (smoked)	90	142 g (5 oz)	440
Pilchards (in oil, canned)	65	113 g (4 oz)	250
Plaice (fried in breadcrumbs)	65	142 g (5 oz)	325
Prawns (boiled and shelled)	30	57 g (2 oz)	60
Salmon (smoked)	40	57 g (2 oz)	80
Salmon (canned)	45	57 g (2 oz)	90
Sardines (in oil, canned)	60	57 g (2 oz)	120
Fish fingers (fried)	65	3 fingers	195

Bread

Bread	Calories per 30 g (1 oz)	Size of average portion	Calories per portion
Bread (wholemeal)	60	30 g (1 oz)	60
Bread (white)	70	30 g (1 oz)	70
Cream crackers	125	1 cracker	40
Pizza (cheese and tomato)	65	1 small	260
Rye crispbread	90	1 biscuit	25

 Spreads

Spread	Calories per 30 g (1 oz)	Size of average portion	Calories per portion
Butter	210	1 pat	50
Honey	80	1 teaspoon	20
Jam	75	1 teaspoon	20
Low-fat spread	105	1 teaspoon	20
Margarine	210	1 teaspoon	50
Marmalade	75	1 teaspoon	20
Peanut butter	175	30 g (1 oz)	175

Cal Salads (raw)

Salad	Calories per 30 g (1 oz)	Size of average portion	Calories per portion
Coleslaw	20	113 g (4 oz)	80
Cucumber	3	30 g (1 oz)	3
Radish	4	30 g (1 oz)	4
Lettuce	3	85 g (3 oz)	10
Tomato	4	1 medium	15

Cal Eggs

Egg	Calories per 30 g (1 oz)	Size of average portion	Calories per portion
Egg (boiled)	40	1 large	80
Egg (fried)	65	1 large	130
Egg (poached)	45	1 large	90
Egg (scrambled)	70	1 large	140

Nuts

Nut	Calories per 30 g (1 oz)	Size of average portion	Calories per portion
Almonds	160	57 g (2 oz)	320
Brazil nuts	175	57 g (2 oz)	350
Cashew nuts	155	113 g (4 oz)	610
Hazelnuts	110	30 g (1 oz)	110
Peanuts	160	30 g (1 oz)	160
Pistachio nuts	170	30 g (1 oz)	170
Walnuts	150	30 g (1 oz)	150

 Soups

Soup	Calories per 30 ml (1 fl oz)	Size of average portion	Calories per portion
Cream of chicken	15	284 ml (1/2 pt)	140
Chicken noodle	5	284 ml (1/2 pt)	55
Minestrone	10	284 ml (1/2 pt)	95
Mushroom	15	284 ml (1/2 pt)	140
Oxtail	15	284 ml (1/2 pt)	140
Tomato	15	284 ml (1/2 pt)	140
Vegetable	10	284 ml (1/2 pt)	95

Cal Cakes and biscuits

Cake or biscuit	Calories per 30 g (1 oz)	Size of average portion	Calories per portion
Cheese cake	120	113 g (4 oz)	430
Chocolate cake (filled and iced)	85	113 g (4 oz)	330
Currant bun (plain)	85	1 bun	340
Currant bun (iced)	90	1 bun	360
Custard tart	95	113 g (4 oz)	370
Danish pastry	105	1 small	210
Digestive biscuit (plain)	135	1 biscuit	70
Digestive biscuit (chocolate)	140	1 biscuit	130
Doughnut (jam)	105	1 doughnut	450
Jam tart	120	1 tart	120
Lardy cake	105	113 g (4 oz)	410
Madeira cake	110	85 g (3 oz)	330
Rich fruit cake	95	85 g (3 oz)	280
Shortbread	145	1 biscuit	95
Sponge cake (with fat)	130	57 g (2 oz)	260
Sponge cake (without fat)	85	57 g (2 oz)	170
Treacle tart	105	113 g (4 oz)	420

Cal Breakfast cereals

Cereal	Calories per 30 g (1 oz)	Size of average portion	Calories per portion
Cornflakes	105	30 g (1 oz)	105
Crisped rice	105	14 g (1/2 oz)	50
Muesli	105	57 g (2 oz)	210
Porridge	110	30 g (1 oz)	110
Puffed wheat	100	30 g (1 oz)	100
Shredded wheat	90	30 g (1 oz)	90

Cal Accompaniments

Accompaniment	Calories per 30 g (1 oz)	Size of average portion	Calories per portion
Rice (boiled)	35	30 g (1 oz)	35
Spaghetti (boiled)	35	170 g (6 oz)	200
Spaghetti (in tomato sauce)	15	170 g (6 oz)	100
Yorkshire pudding	60	1 small	120

Cal Pulses (boiled, unless otherwise stated)

Pulse	Calories per 30 g (1 oz)	Size of average portion	Calories per portion
Chickpeas	40	113 g (4 oz)	160
Lentils	25	113 g (4 oz)	105

Cal Puddings

Pudding	Calories per 30 g (1 oz)	Size of average portion	Calories per portion
Apple crumble	60	227 g (8 oz)	480
Apple pie	50	170 g (6 oz)	300
Custard	35	142 g (5 oz)	170
Ice cream (non-dairy)	45	57 g (2 oz)	90
Jelly (fruit)	15	113 g (4 oz)	60
Sponge pudding	100	113 g (4 oz)	400
Suet pudding	95	142 g (5 oz)	475
Trifle	45	170 g (6 oz)	270
Yogurt (fruit)	30	small carton	135

Cal Miscellaneous food

Miscellaneous food	Calories per 30 g (1 oz)	Size of average portion	Calories per portion
Mayonnaise	145	30 g (1 oz)	145
Sugar	120	1 teaspoon (5 g)	20

Much more information on specific foods and their calorie content is available in *Collins Gem Calorie Counter*.

3. Cleaning and clothing

CLEANING TOOLS AND STORAGE
It is always a good idea to have cleaning tools at the ready. For this reason, it is best to keep them stored neatly and where they are easily accessible. Don't go out and buy tools and cleaning agents for the sake of it, but when you do buy, buy with the future in mind. This way you may save some money and end up with a better stocked store of cleaning tools and products.

Remember that cleaning agents are potentially harmful and should be kept out of the reach of children.

This list is an indication of items you should keep in your store:

- Broom – soft bristled
- Broom – hard bristled
- Dustpan and brush
- Hard bristled scrubbing brush
- Soft hand brush
- Toilet brush (for each toilet)
- Dust mop
- Long handled dust mop (for ceilings and cobwebs)
- Floor mop (detachable head type)
- Bucket (double compartment type)
- Chamois leather
- Cleaning cloths (old clothes, sheets, towels)
- Cleaning products
- Rubber gloves
- Scouring pads
- Sponges (various sizes)
- Squeegee (for cleaning windows)
- Stepladder
- Vacuum cleaner
- Waxes
- Polishes
- Oils (various types for different uses)

LAUNDRY CODES

Most garments contain a label giving laundering instructions, usually shown in terms of symbols, that tell you if any item is washable (or should be dry-cleaned) and how to wash it. The codes are listed below.

The table on the following pages lists the old and new codes, recommended temperatures (for machine- or hand-washing), and other machine settings, and the types of fabric that should be washed according to that code.

a machine or hand wash
b can be bleached
c do not bleach
d iron
e do not iron

f dry-cleanable
g do not dry-clean
h tumble dry
i do not tumble dry

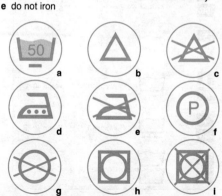

Laundry codes and their meanings

| Code | | Temperature | |
Old	New	Machine wash	Hand wash
1 9 95 95		Very hot 95 °C to boil	Hand hot 50 °C or boil
2 3 60 60		Hot 60 °C	Hand hot 50 °C
4 50		Hand hot 50 °C	Hand hot 50 °C
5 40		Warm 40 °C	Warm 40 °C
6 40		Warm 40 °C	Warm 40 °C
7 40		Warm 40 °C	Warm 40 °C
8 30		Cool 30 °C	Cool 30 °C

Agitation	Rinse	Spin	Fabric
Maximum	Normal	Normal	White cotton and linen with no special finish
Maximum	Normal	Normal	Cotton, linen, viscose, colourfast with no special finish
Medium	Cold	Short spin or drip dry	Coloured nylon, polyester, cotton and viscose with special finish
Maximum	Normal	Normal	Cotton, linen, viscose, colourfast to 40 °C
Minimum	Cold	Short spin	Acrylics, acetate and mixtures with wool
Minimum; do not rub	Normal	Normal; do not hand wring	Wool and wool mixtures
Minimum	Cold	Short spin; do not hand wring	Silk and printed acetate, not colourfast at 40 °C

FABRIC CARE

These are general guidelines for washing and drying clothing of most fabric types. Whenever

Fabric	Method of cleaning
Acetate	Dry-clean or hand wash gently. Do not wring. Drip dry and iron at a cool setting when still damp.
Acrylic	Machine wash and tumble dry. Turning inside out for washing reduces fabric wear. Jumpers won't shrink, but drying them flat helps them keep their shape. Use a cool iron if necessary.
Cotton	Machine wash whites in hot or warm water, with bleach if desired; colourfast fabrics in warm water; non-colourfast in cold. Tumble or hang dry. Iron at hot setting. Cotton shrinks in first few washings, unless it is preshrunk fabric, as in many jeans. Turning jeans inside out for washing reduces fading.
Linen	Dry-clean. If label indicates washable, hand or machine wash (delicate cycle). Drip dry and iron on reverse side of fabric while damp.
Nylon	Hand wash tights and drip dry. Hand or machine wash other nylon fabrics in warm water. Drip or tumble dry, and iron on cool setting if necessary.

possible, follow the manufacturer's instructions on the garment's label.

Fabric	Method of cleaning
Polyester	Machine wash; tumble dry. Use warm iron if necessary.
Rayon	Dry-clean. If label indicates washable, hand wash in mild soap and warm water. Do not wring. Tumble or drip dry. Use warm iron while fabric is damp.
Silk	Dry-clean. If, however, the garment label displays Ⓕ, dry-cleaning is unsuitable. If label indicates washable, hand wash in mild soap and cool water. Roll in towel, then drip dry. Use cool iron while fabric is damp.
Wool	Dry-clean. If label indicates washable, hand wash in mild soap and cool water. Do not wring, but gently squeeze out excess moisture (or run it through the washer's spin cycle) and dry flat, on a towel. Jumpers can also be machine-washed in mild soap. Squeeze out moisture after rinsing (or run it through the washer's rinse and spin cycles), then dry flat on a towel.

CLOTHING SIZES

UK clothing sizes are equal to US sizes for some items, such as children's shoes; for others, the two vary slightly. Below are listed the European equivalents of UK and US clothing and shoe sizes. Remember also that sizes vary depending on the manufacturers.

Men's shoes

UK	USA	Europe
$6^1/_2$	7	39
7	$7^1/_2$	40
$7^1/_2$	8	41
8	$8^1/_2$	42
$8^1/_2$	9	43
9	$9^1/_2$	43
$9^1/_2$	10	44
10	$10^1/_2$	44
$10^1/_2$	11	45

Children's shoes

UK/USA	Europe
0	15
1	17
2	18
3	19
4	20
$4^1/_2$	21
5	22
6	23
7	24
8	25
$8^1/_2$	26
9	27
10	28
11	29
12	30
$12^1/_2$	31
13	32

Women's shoes

UK	USA	Europe
$3^1/_2$	5	36
$4^1/_2$	6	37
$5^1/_2$	7	38
$6^1/_2$	8	39
$7^1/_2$	9	40

Men's suits/overcoats

UK/USA	Europe
36	46
38	48
40	50
42	52
44	54
46	56

Men's shirts

UK/USA	Europe
12	30–31
12½	32
13	33
13½	34–35
14	36
14½	37
15	38
15½	39–40
16	41
16½	42
17	43
17½	44–45

Men's socks

UK/USA	Europe
9	38–39
10	39–40
10½	40–41
11	41–42
11½	42–43

Women's clothing

UK	USA	Europe
8	6	36
10	8	38
12	10	40
14	12	42
16	14	44
18	16	46
20	18	48
22	20	50
24	22	52

Children's clothing

UK	USA	Europe
16–18	2	40–45
20–22	4	50–55
24–26	6	60–65
28–30	7	70–75
32–34	8	80–85
36–38	9	90–95

BODY MEASUREMENTS

The standard body measurements shown on the diagram on the opposite page are those needed for garment fitting.

Below are a few tips on taking some of these measurements.

Neck
Measure at the fullest part.

Chest/bust
Measure at the fullest part of the bust or chest and straight across back.

Waist
Tie a string around the thinnest part of your body (the waist) and leave it there as a point of reference for other measurements.

Hips
There are two places to measure hips, depending on the garment: one is 5–10 cm (2–4 in) below the waist, at the top of the hipbones; the other is at the fullest part, usually 18–23 cm (7–9 in) below.

Arm
Measure at the fullest part, usually about 2.5 cm (1 in) below the armpit.

Arm length
Start at the shoulder bone and continue past the elbow to the wrist, with the arm slightly bent.

Back
Measure from the prominent bone in the back of the neck down the centre to the waist string.

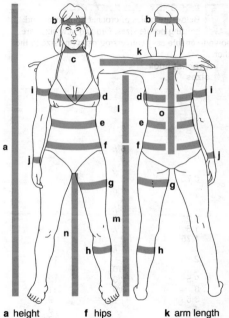

a height
b head
c neck
d chest/bust
e waist
f hips
g thigh
h calf
i arm
j wrist
k arm length
l armpit to hip
m outside leg
n inside leg
o back

CROCHET AND KNITTING

Below are tables of crochet hook sizes and knitting needle sizes. Old and new sizes are shown to enable easy conversion from one size to the other.

Crochet hook sizes

New international range	Old steel size	Old aluminium size
	8	
	7	
	6½	
0.6	6	
	5½	
0.75	5	
	4½	
1	4	
	3½	
1.25	3	
1.5	2½	
1.75	2	
	1½	
2	1	14
	1/0	
2.5	2/0	12
3	3/0	11
3.5		9
4		8
4.5		7
5		6
5.5		5
6		4
7		2

5 Knitting needle sizes

New metric size (mm)	Old size	New metric size (mm)	Old size
10.00	000	4.50	7
9.00	00	4.00	8
8.00	0	3.75	9
7.50	1	3.25	10
7.00	2	3.00	11
6.50	3	2.75	12
6.00	4	2.15	13
5.50	5	2.00	14
5.00	6		

Here, the old British system is shown in colour, and the American numbering system in black.

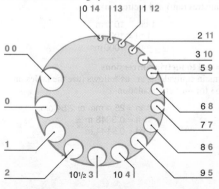

4. Decorating and DIY

USEFUL MEASURES
The following conversions and unit equivalents
will help you with your decorating and DIY.

LENGTH
Imperial units
Imperial units are measured in inches (in), feet
(ft), yards (yd) and chains (ch).

$$1 \text{ ft} = 12 \text{ in}$$
$$1 \text{ yd} = 3 \text{ ft}$$
$$1 \text{ ch} = 22 \text{ yd}$$

Metric units
Metric units are measured in millimetres (mm),
centimetres (cm) and metres (m).

$$1 \text{ cm} = 10 \text{ mm}$$
$$1 \text{ m} = 100 \text{ cm}$$
$$1 \text{ m} = 1000 \text{ mm}$$

Imperial to metric conversions
The main equivalents are as follows (use the tables on
p. 163 for further calculations):

$$1 \text{ in} = 25.4 \text{ mm or } 2.54 \text{ cm}$$
$$1 \text{ ft} = 0.3048 \text{ m}$$
$$1 \text{ yd} = 0.9144 \text{ m}$$

Metric to imperial conversions
The main equivalents are as follows (use the tables on
p. 164 for further calculations):

$$1 \text{ mm} = 0.039 \text{ in}$$
$$1 \text{ cm} = 0.3937 \text{ in}$$
$$1 \text{ m} = 39.37 \text{ in or } 3.2808 \text{ ft}$$

AREA
Imperial units
Imperial units are measured in square inches
(sq in), square feet (sq ft) and square yards (sq yd).

$$1 \text{ sq ft} = 144 \text{ sq in}$$
$$1 \text{ sq yd} = 9 \text{ sq ft}$$

Metric units
Metric units are measured in square centimetres (sq cm)
and square metres (sq m).

$$1 \text{ sq m} = 10 \ 000 \text{ sq cm}$$

Imperial to metric conversions
The main equivalents are as follows (use the tables on
p. 166 for further calculations):

$$1 \text{ sq in} = 645.2 \text{ sq mm or } 6.452 \text{ sq cm}$$
$$1 \text{ sq ft} = 0.093 \text{ sq m}$$
$$1 \text{ sq yd} = 0.836 \text{ sq m}$$

Metric to imperial conversions

The main equivalents are as follows (use the tables on p. 167 for further calculations):

$$1 \text{ sq mm} = 0.0016 \text{ sq in}$$
$$1 \text{ sq cm} = 0.155 \text{ sq in}$$
$$1 \text{ sq m} = 10.764 \text{ sq ft or } 1.196 \text{ sq yd}$$

DECORATING COLOUR GUIDE

There are many ways of combining colours in the home to produce a pleasing effect. The way you combine colours can set the mood. For example, reds, oranges and yellows tend to create warmth; blues, greens and purples help create coolness and tranquillity. Colours also help increase or decrease the 'apparent' size of a room. For example, light-coloured walls, floors and ceilings can make dark, poky rooms appear larger; dark colours used in the same way can make large, cold rooms feel cosier and more welcoming. Use the suggestions below and the colour wheel opposite to help you choose the effect you want to create.

Single colour ('monochromatic') schemes

In schemes of this sort, the walls and furnishings are shades and tints of a single colour, such as blue. They are the simplest schemes to start with and are very effective.

Schemes of related colours

For a scheme of this type, use two or three colours near each other on the colour wheel. For example, you could blend yellow, green and blue or red, orange and yellow.

The colour wheel

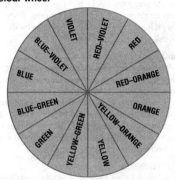

Schemes of complementary colours

These are colours directly opposite one another, or nearly so, on the colour wheel; for example, red and green or orange and blue. Such schemes work best if one colour predominates and the other provides accents. Complementary colours are tricky to balance, so test them out first in small amounts, using cushions and wallhangings, for example.

Schemes of three colours (triad)

These are three colours at equal distances apart on the colour wheel. For example, blue, red and yellow. Wallpaper or fabrics could contain all three colours, set against a plain background, such as a dark blue carpet.

Schemes of neutral colours

Black, white and grey can be used as background to or
to accentuate most bright or pastel colours. Browns and
beiges, which are between red and yellow on the colour
wheel, work well with tones in that range.

Hints and tips

- Take the colours of a favourite rug, vase, poster or
  painting, and use these as a basis for your colour
  scheme.
- Fabric samples and colour swatches can be mixed and
  matched on a sheet of paper to create a chosen effect.
- Get a paint supplier to mix and match paint to your
  precise requirements. Take along samples of fabric or
  floor coverings to get the right match.

 PAINTING

A bewildering variety of paints is available.
Different surfaces, different finishes and
different conditions require different paints.

Constituents of paint

There are three basic parts to any paint:

- the pigment provides the colour and covering power;
- the binder holds the pigment together and bonds it to
  the painted surface; and
- the liquid carrier holds the pigment and binder. It
  dries or evaporates and leaves the other two parts
  behind on the painted surface.

Surface finishes

Paints come in several types of surface finish: matt
(dull); gloss (shiny); and semi-gloss (with a sheen) –
silk, satin, eggshell, and so on.

Which paint to use?

Despite the vast array of paint types, when it comes to most decorating jobs, the choices can be narrowed down quickly.

For **outside walls**, there are exterior-grade emulsion, gloss, cement, masonry and clear, water-repellent paints. Whitewash is a cheap option, but a heavy coating is needed to seal walls from moisture and dirt.

For **wood and metal**, indoors or out, an oil-based gloss paint as the final surface (topcoat) is best. Stripped or new wood, and metals which rust or corrode, should be treated with a primer, then an undercoat, and finally one or more topcoats.

For **indoor walls and ceilings**, a water-based emulsion paint is normally used. Use two or three coats. For other situations, refer to the chart on the following pages.

How much paint do you need?

Paints are sold in metric quantities, which roughly correspond with imperial sizes:

> 500 ml is slightly less than 1 pint (pt)
> 1 litre (l) is slightly less than 1 quart (qt)
> 5 l is slightly more than 1 gallon (gal)

When calculating how much paint you need to buy, you need to know three things:

- an estimate of the area you want to paint;
- the paint manufacturer's estimate of the area the paint will cover; and
- the number of coats of paint you need to apply.

Easy-to-follow steps for calculating the area you want to paint and how much paint you need start on p. 122.

Surfaces and suitable coatings guide

The chart is easy to use. Read down the left-hand column to find the surface you wish to paint. Then look across the row, from left to right, to find

Surface (previous covering)	Shellac knotting	Wood primer (white)	Aluminium wood primer	Multipurpose primer	Zinc chromate primer	Alkali-resisting primers	Masonry sealer
Wallpaper				●			
Canvas and hessian				●			
Polystyrene				●			
Alkyd matt and eggshell							
Alkyd gloss							
Emulsion vinyl or acrylic				●			
Emulsion exterior							●
Polyurethane gloss or varnish							
Metallic paint							
Cement paint							●
Masonry paint				●			
Wood preservative							
Wood stain		●	●				

which sealer or primer is required (if any), which
undercoat is needed, and which topcoats are
recommended.

Undercoats			Topcoats												
Alkyd undercoat	Epoxy undercoat	Polyurethane undercoat	Alkyd liquid gloss	Alkyd gel gloss	Emulsion vinyl or acrylic (liquid or gel)	Alkyd eggshell	Emulsion exterior	Polyurethane paint	Cement paint	Floor paint	Metallic paint	Masonry paint	Alkyd varnish	Spar varnish	Polyurethane varnish
					•										
					•										
					•										
•	•	•	•	•	•			•			•				
•	•	•	•	•	•			•			•				
•	•	•	•	•	•			•			•				
								•							
•	•	•	•	•	•			•					•	•	•
•	•	•	•	•	•			•					•	•	•
									•						
						•		•							
													•	•	•
•	•	•	•	•	•			•				•	•	•	•

continued

Surfaces and suitable coatings guide (continued)

Surface	Coating	Shellac knotting	Wood primer (white)	Aluminium wood primer	Multipurpose primer	Zinc chromate primer	Alkali-resisting primers	Masonry sealer
Raw wood								
Softwood		•	•	•	•			
Hardwood		•		•	•			
Plywood			•	•	•			
Hardboard			•		•			
Raw masonry								
New plaster					•		•	
Gypsum plaster					•		•	
Concrete							•	•
Cement render							•	•
Brickwork							•	•
Concrete floors							•	
Bare metal								
Iron and steel						•		
Galvanized iron						•		
Aluminium						•		

Alkyd undercoat	Epoxy undercoat	Polyurethane undercoat	Alkyd liquid gloss	Alkyd gel gloss	Emulsion vinyl or acrylic (liquid or gel)	Alkyd eggshell	Emulsion exterior	Polyurethane paint	Cement paint	Floor paint	Metallic paint	Masonry paint	Alkyd varnish	Spar varnish	Polyurethane varnish
							Undercoats			Topcoats					
•	•	•	•	•		•		•					•	•	•
•	•	•	•	•		•		•					•	•	•
•	•	•	•	•		•		•					•	•	•
•	•	•	•	•		•		•							•
•			•	•		•		•							
•			•		•										
			•	•	•		•	•	•			•			
			•	•	•		•	•				•			
•			•	•	•	•	•	•				•			
										•					
•	•	•	•					•				•			
•	•	•	•					•				•			
•	•	•	•					•			•				

Calculating the area you want to paint
Easy-to-follow steps are outlined below, together with a
worked example to guide you.
1 Measure the height and width of each wall.
2 Round each value up to the nearest 0.1 m.

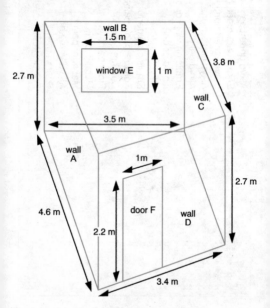

3 Multiply each wall's height and width together:

> area of wall A = 2.7 × 4.6 = 12.4 sq m
> area of wall B = 2.7 × 3.5 = 9.5 sq m
> area of wall C = 2.7 × 3.8 = 10.3 sq m
> area of wall D = 2.7 × 3.4 = 9.2 sq m

4 Add the areas together:

> total area of walls A, B, C and D
> = 12.4 + 9.5 + 10.3 + 9.2 = 41.4 sq m

5 Measure the height and width of any doors, windows and other features which you are not going to paint (as before, round to the nearest 0.1 m).
6 For each feature, multiply the two figures together to arrive at an area for each:

> area of window E = 1 × 1.5 = 1.5 sq m
> area of door F = 2.2 × 1 = 2.2 sq m

7 Add the areas together:

> total area of the features to be left unpainted
> = 1.5 + 2.2 = 3.7 sq m

8 Subtract the areas of unpainted features from the total areas of the walls to give you the total area to be painted.

> total area of walls = 41.4 sq m
> total unpainted areas = 3.7 sq m
>
> area to be painted = 41.4 − 3.7 = 37.7 sq m

Calculating how much paint you need

Continuing with the worked example from before, steps for working out how much paint you need are outlined below.

1 Divide the area to be painted by the covering capacity of the paint. This will give you the number of litres you require for one coat of paint:

area to be painted = 37.7 sq m
covering capacity of liquid emulsion paint
= 15 sq m per litre

one coat requires 37.7 ÷ 15 sq m per litre

2 To discover how many litres you will need for more than one coat, multiply the number of litres for one coat by the number of coats to be applied:

one coat requires 2.5 l
two coats require 2.5 × 2 = 5 l

The table opposite gives estimates for the covering capacities of different paints (paint covering capacities vary slightly from one manufacturer to another).

Basic rules for preparing and painting a room

- The walls and ceiling should be prepared before the woodwork is tackled.
- Preparation creates dust, so you should complete any preparation before painting. The exception is if you use wet abrasive paper, which does not create dust. For example, you can use this to remove specks of emulsion paint from woodwork before painting it.

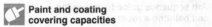

Paint and coating covering capacities

Coating	Smooth surface		Rough surface	
	Sq m per litre	Sq ft per litre	Sq m per litre	Sq ft per litre
Aluminium wood primer	15	160		
Multipurpose primer	15	160	4	45
Wood primer (white)	15	160	9	100
Zinc chromate Primer Undercoat	16 19	170 200	11	115
Liquid gloss paint	15	160		
Gel gloss paint	11	115		
Liquid emulsion	15	160	4	45
Gel emulsion	11	115	4	45

Job sequence guide for preparing and painting a room

Ceiling and walls	Woodwork
1 Remove wallpaper (only necessary if the wallpaper is heavily patterned and difficult to cover or is unsound and will colour-run or bubble on painting. Test by painting a small area first).	
2 Strip any loose or flaking paint.	
3 Rub down any gloss painted surfaces.	
4 Wash down all painted surfaces (ceiling then walls).	
5 Fill cracks and holes.	
	6 Strip if paint is loose or flaking.
7 Prime any bare (untreated) surfaces.	

Ceiling and walls	Woodwork
	8 Fill and prime any bare wood.
9 Paint ceiling.	
	10 Rub down all paintwork with wet abrasive paper.
	11 Fill any holes, dents or cracks and then **smooth** with wet abrasive paper.
12 Paint walls.	
	13 Paint woodwork.
14 Paint ceiling (second coat).	
15 Paint walls (second coat).	
	16 Paint woodwork (second coat).

WALLPAPERING

Types of wallpaper and their uses

Type	Uses
Lining paper	For lining a rough or uneven wall before painting or papering. For covering a painted wall before papering.
Embossed paper such as Anaglypta, Supaglypta and woodchip	For covering particularly rough or uneven surfaces before painting.
Standard wallpaper	The most commonly used wallpaper for general use. The paper is patterned and, unlike ready-pasted wallpaper, it requires pasting before hanging.

How much wallpaper do you need?

Most wallpaper is sold in rolls 10.05 m (11 yd) long and 53 cm (21 in) wide.

To calculate how many rolls of wallpaper you need to paper a room, follow the steps given below.

1 Measure the distance around the room (the width of all the walls added together). Include doors and windows.

Type	Uses
Ready-pasted wallpaper	As standard wallpaper but requires wetting rather than pasting before hanging.
Vinyl wallcovering	A thick pvc-coated wallcovering. It is waterproof, scrubbable and easy to hang after pasting. It is particularly suitable for kitchens, bathrooms and children's rooms.
Ready-pasted vinyl wallcovering	As vinyl wallcovering but requires wetting rather than pasting before hanging.

2 Measure the height from skirting board to ceiling.
3 Now refer to the charts on the next page to find out how many rolls you need. Add an extra roll if the wallpaper pattern you have chosen is a large one, and you need to align one drop with the next.

Number of rolls of wallpaper required: metric estimator

The number of rolls required, according to room circumference and wall height (shown in colour), is shown in black.

Room Circumference (m)	1.80–2.15	2.15–2.30	2.30–2.45	2.45–2.60	2.60–2.75	2.75–2.90	2.90–3.00
9	4	4	5	5	5	5	6
10	5	5	5	5	6	6	6
11	5	5	6	6	6	7	7
12	5	6	6	6	7	7	7
13	6	6	7	7	7	8	8
14	6	7	7	7	8	8	8
15	7	7	7	8	8	9	9
16	7	7	8	8	9	9	10
17	7	8	8	9	9	10	10
18	8	8	9	9	10	10	11
19	8	9	9	10	10	11	11
20	9	9	10	10	11	11	12
21	9	10	10	11	11	12	12
22	9	10	11	11	12	13	13

Wall height (m) shown across top columns.

Number of rolls of wallpaper required: imperial estimator

The number of rolls required, according to room circumference and wall height (shown in colour), is shown in black.

Room Circumference (ft)	Wall height (ft and in)						
	6'0"–7'0"	7'0"–7'6"	7'6"–8'0"	8'0"–8'6"	8'6"–9'0"	9'0"–9'6"	9'6"–10'0"
30	4	4	5	5	5	5	6
33	5	5	5	5	6	6	6
36	5	5	6	6	6	7	7
39	5	6	6	6	7	7	7
43	6	6	7	7	7	8	8
46	6	7	7	7	8	8	8
49	7	7	7	8	8	9	9
52	7	7	8	8	9	9	10
56	7	8	8	9	9	10	10
59	8	8	9	9	10	10	11
62	8	9	9	10	10	11	11
66	9	9	10	10	11	11	12
69	9	10	10	11	11	12	12
73	9	10	11	11	12	13	13

Preparation for wallpapering

As with painting, the trick is to do enough preparation to achieve the results you want, but not to do any unnecessary work. Preparation is hard work and time-consuming.

The aim is to produce a surface which is clean, dry and flat, and to which the wallpaper paste will adhere. How you achieve this depends on the type of existing surface.

Old wallpaper Paper over this only if it is smooth and sound. Otherwise it will need to be stripped. You can do this by soaking and stripping or using a steam stripper. Fill any cracks and holes in the stripped wall and sand smooth.

Old Plaster Fill cracks and holes and then sand smooth. Apply a coat of size before papering.

New plaster Should be left for at least 6 months before papering. Treat with primer/sealer before papering.

Plasterboard Treat with primer/sealer before papering.

Emulsion paint Wash down until clean and all loosely adhered paint is removed.

Gloss paint Rub down with coarse glasspaper to form a flat, keyed (roughened) surface to which the paste will adhere.

Job sequence guide for wallpapering a room

Wallpapering sequence

1 **Protect the room contents** by removing as much furniture as possible, rolling back the carpet or covering it and any remaining furniture with dustsheets.

2 **Prepare the wall surfaces** so that they are smooth, dry and sound (see p. 132).

3 **Cut the wallpaper** into correctly measured lengths, 10 cm (4 in) longer than the measured height to be papered.

4 **Paste and fold** the wallpaper one strip at a time. Carry the folded wallpaper strip to the wall.

5 **Position the wallpaper strip** vertically, overlapping both the ceiling and skirting board by about 5 cm (2 in).

6 **Brush the wallpaper smooth** from centre to edges, progressing from the top of the strip to the bottom.

7 **Trim the top and bottom edges** to length.

8 **Continue with steps 4–7 for the next strip of paper** butted alongside the first. Ensure that the wallpaper pattern, where present, is aligned between one strip and the next.

TILING

Types of tile and their uses

Type	Uses
Ceramic (plain or patterned, smooth or textured)	The tiles are durable, and stain- and water-resistant. They are a good choice for kitchens and bathrooms.
Heat-resistant or ceramic	Use around a fireplace, boiler or cooker.
Mosaic (ceramic tiles mounted on a sheet of paper or mesh)	Useful for tiling small or awkwardly shaped areas. Expensive.
Plastic (thin tiles with the appearance of ceramic tiles)	Easier to cut and mount than ceramic tiles, but they are much less durable and less scratch-resistant. Warm to the touch.
Mirror (squares of silvered glass)	Useful for increasing the apparent size of a room. The wall must be perfectly flat or the reflection will be distorted.

Type	Uses
Cork	Provide good heat and sound insulation in large areas. They are not very durable and they are liable to damage by abrasion. But they are lightweight and relatively easy to mount.
Ceiling (polystyrene)	Provide good heat and sound insulation. Inexpensive, light-weight and easy to fix, they should not be used in the kitchen or other areas where they pose a fire hazard.
Ceiling (fibre)	As for polystyrene ceiling tiles. The edges are usually tongue-and-grooved. An interlocked sheet can be pinned to the ceiling joists.

Tile shapes and sizes

Ceramic tiles are usually square or rectangular. Some common sizes are shown below. The smaller sizes are usually 4 mm ($^5/_{32}$ in) thick, while larger tiles may be 6 mm ($^1/_4$ in) or more in thickness.

Tile sizes

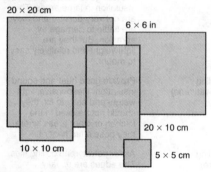

20 × 20 cm

6 × 6 in

20 × 10 cm

10 × 10 cm

5 × 5 cm

How many tiles do you need?

Easy-to-follow steps are outlined below, together with a worked example to guide you.

1 Measure the height and width of the area to be covered.
2 Multiply the two values together. For example:

> region to be tiled is 2 m high by 3 m wide
> area to be tiled = 2 × 3 = 6 sq m
> or
> region to be tiled is 6 ft high by 10 ft wide
> area to be tiled = 6 × 10 = 60 sq ft

3 Measure the height and width of a tile.

4 Multiply the two values together. For example:

tile is 20 cm by 20 cm
area of tile = 20 × 20 = 400 sq cm
or
tile is 6 in by 6 in
area of tile = 6 × 6 = 36 sq in

5 Make sure that the tile area and the area to be covered are converted to the same units. Convert the larger units to the smaller ones.

1 sq m = 100 cm × 100 cm = 10 000 sq cm

1 sq ft = 12 in × 12 in = 144 sq in

so an area of 6 sq m = 6 × 10 000 sq cm
= 60 000 sq cm

an area of 60 sq ft = 60 × 144 sq in
= 8640 sq in

6 Divide the area to be covered by the area of a tile to give the number of tiles needed. For example:

the number of tiles needed
for an area of 6 sq m = 60 000 ÷ 400 = 150

the number of tiles needed
for an area of 60 sq ft = 8640 ÷ 36 = 240

7 Add on about 10% to your final tile count to allow for breakages and for any cut tiles.

Tile arrangements

Tile arrangements are not always simple. Sometimes there will be features such as cupboards or windows which you will have to tile around. You may wish to make a patterned arrangement, in which case you will probably have to buy tiles of more than one type.

Planning a tile arrangement

1 Plan on graph paper, using one square on the paper to represent one tile (or two squares to represent a rectangular tile). Use a separate sheet of graph paper for each wall or area you want to tile.

2 Work out the scale. For example, if you are using 1 cm square graph paper and the tiles are 10 cm × 10 cm, then 1 cm on the graph paper equals 10 cm of tile.

3 On tracing paper, draw to scale the shape of the area to be covered. For example, an area 2 m × 3 m will be 20 cm × 30 cm on the graph paper.

4 Measure any features, such as windows or cupboards,

Planning on graph paper

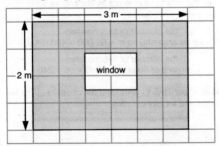

which lie within the area to be tiled. Put these features
on the plan.

5 Place the tracing paper over the graph paper.

6 By moving the tracing paper around, decide on the
best arrangement of tiles which will cover the marked
area. Aim to make the tile arrangement symmetrical
and exclude any cut tiles which are less than 2.5 cm
(1 in) across.

7 When you have decided on the best arrangement,
trace the area outline onto the graph paper and then go
over the outline in ink.

8 On the graph paper, mark the position of any tiles
which have special patterns.

9 Apart from the field tiles (whose edges are all flat and
unglazed), which may make up the bulk of your
arrangement, you will need to count the number of tiles
with glazed, rounded edges (RE) that you need for the
borders of the tiled area. You will also need to count the
number of tiles with adjacent glazed, rounded edges
(REX) needed for the corners.

Preparation for tiling

The aim is to produce a surface which is dry, level and
grease-free, and to which the tiling adhesive will
readily stick.

The surface must be rigid and be capable of supporting
the sometimes considerable weight of the tiles.

How you will achieve the above depends on the
existing surface.

Wallpaper Wallpaper and other wallcoverings need to
be removed. Once they are removed, wash down the
revealed plaster or plasterboard with water.

Gloss paint Use a strip of adhesive tape to check whether the paint is firmly bonded to the wall. If the paint pulls away, the surface will have to be removed or covered with plywood before tiling. If the paint is basically sound, scrape off any loose paint and prime bare patches. Wash down and then rub the whole area with coarse glasspaper.

Emulsion paint Wash down the area.

Plaster This is a suitable surface for tiling provided it is at least 6 weeks old. Ensure by filling and sanding that the plaster is smooth and flat. Apply a primer/sealer before tiling.

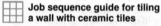

Job sequence guide for tiling a wall with ceramic tiles

1 **Protect the room's contents** by removing or covering furniture and rolling back or covering the carpet.

2 **Prepare the wall surfaces** so that they are smooth, dry and sound (see previous page and above).

3 **Fix a straight batten horizontally** across the bottom of the area to be tiled. Use perfectly straight 5 cm × 2.5 cm (2 in × 1 in) battening, masonry nails for fixing and a spirit level to ensure that the batten is horizontal.

4 **Set up a vertical line** in the centre of the area, using a plumb line.

Wood Wood sheeting, plywood, hardboard and
chipboard sheets are a suitable tiling surface provided
they are flat and are firmly attached to the wall. Use a
flexible tile adhesive. Narrow wooden strips are not a
suitable surface.

Brick Provided it is smooth and dry it can be a suitable
surface. Usually, however, brick walls are too rough
and need to be lined with plywood before tiling.

Tiles Existing tiles make a satisfactory base provided
they are sound. Rub down with a suitable abrasive
paper and wash down thoroughly before tiling.

---

5 **Begin tiling from the base upwards** (see p.142)
   using whole tiles. Check that the tiles are properly
   aligned both vertically and horizontally.

6 **Remove the batten** after leaving the tiles to dry
   for 8–12 hours.

7 **Cut corner and edge tiles to size** and then fit.

8 **Leave the tiles to dry** for a further 8–12 hours.

9 **Use grouting** to fill in spaces between the tiles.

10 **Allow the grouting to dry** and then polish the
   surface of the tiles with a soft cloth.

Tiling sequences

Numbers show sequence in which tiles are mounted.

Running bond

Staggers the tiles. Place the first one centrally on your vertical line.

14	10	18		
13	6	9	17	
12	4	5	8	16
11	2	1	3	7	15

Jack-on-Jack

Has the joints lined up. Work either side of your vertical line.

		13		
	12	7	14	
	11	6	4	8	15
10	5	2	1	3	9	16

Diamond bond

Puts plain or outlined tiles at an angle. Place the first centrally on the vertical, fill in the 'triangles' last.

CURTAIN FABRIC
To calculate how much fabric is required for curtains, first determine the length, then the width of the area you wish to cover.

Length

1 Measure the height of the window from the curtain rod to the floor (or the level you wish the curtains to reach).
2 Add approximately 25 cm for finishing both the top and bottom hems.

Width

1 For gathered curtains, measure the width of your window and multiply by 2.
2 Add 5 cm for each side hem of each curtain, whether you are going to have one, two or more curtains.
3 Most fabrics come in a standard width (often 1.2 m), so you may need two lengths of fabric to make one curtain.
4 Divide the total width by the standard width to see how many lengths you will require.

Calculating the amount of fabric you need

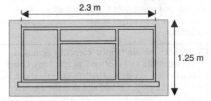

1 The length of the curtain for the window shown above is

$$1.25 \text{ m} + 25 \text{ cm} = 1.50 \text{ m}$$

2 The width required is

$$2.3 \text{ m} \times 2 = 4.6 \text{ m} + 20 \text{ cm (for two curtains)} = 4.8 \text{ m}$$

3 For standard 1.2 m-width fabric, divide this width by
1.2:

$$4.8 \div 1.2 = 4$$

4 The total amount of fabric you will need is four 1.5 m
lengths of fabric:

$$4 \times 1.5 = 6$$
You will need 6 m of fabric

> *Note:* If using patterned material, make sure that
> where the lengths are joined the pattern matches up.
> (You might have to buy extra fabric to allow for this.)

 CARPETS
Calculating the actual amount of carpet needed
for a particular space is a job for a professional
carpet fitter, especially if the space is irregularly
shaped. But being able to make an approximate
estimate of your carpet needs will help in planning and
budgeting.

> *Note:* Like curtain fabrics, carpeting comes in
> standard width sizes (often 2 m and 3 m). Other
> factors, such as pile and pattern direction, can affect
> the way the carpet is laid and thus the amount
> needed.

Measuring and budgeting for carpets
Always measure for the maximum amount of carpet
required, even if it means that some carpet will be
wasted, and remember to include doorway spaces.

1 Measure the room to be carpeted, making a rough plan and noting your measurements on it (see below).

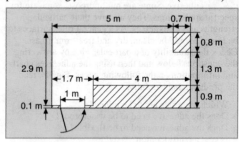

2 Calculate the maximum width and length that are required to cover the space. In this case:

maximum width = 3 m
maximum length = 1.7 + 4 = 5.7 m

3 Multiply the maximum length by the maximum width. In this case:

$$3 \times 5.7 = 17.1 \text{ sq m}$$

4 For budgeting purposes, you can now estimate the costs of the carpet by multiplying this figure by the price per square metre. For example:

$$17.1 \times £13 = £222.30$$

USING ADHESIVES

There is no such thing as an all-purpose adhesive. Some are multipurpose, some are for specific applications. They all have their particular strengths and weaknesses. As a general rule, surfaces to be joined should be clean, dry and free from grease. Check the suitability of a particular glue by answering the questions below and then using the adhesives chart and information on the following pages. Finally, read the product label carefully.

- Which materials are to be joined?
- Does the adhesive need to be waterproof?
- Does the adhesive need to be flexible?
- Is cost a consideration?
- Does drying time need to be short?
- What are the health and safety considerations?

General-purpose adhesives kit

Glues to include in a general purpose adhesives kit are: **PVA adhesive** for woodwork and furniture repairs; **epoxy resin adhesives** for a slow-setting but strong bond in most situations; and for a quick-setting bond, **superglue** (for strength) or a **contact adhesive** (for economy).

Types of adhesive

1 Natural (animal and fish) glue An old-fashioned glue used on tight wood-working joints. Slow-drying, smelly and weakened by damp. Now almost entirely replaced by modern synthetic glues.

2 PVA adhesives A white liquid which dries clear in less than an hour. Used for tight wood-working joints indoors. Weakened by damp and stress. Trade names include Bostik 8, Evostik Wood Adhesive and Unibond.

3 Urea-formaldehyde adhesive A two-part adhesive which is the best choice for exterior woodwork. It is waterproof, resistant to stress and has good filling properties, so that it is useful for filling loose joints. Slow-drying. Trade names include Aerolite and Cascamite.

4 Contact adhesives Based on synthetic rubber, these adhesives are applied to both surfaces, allowed to dry, and the surfaces are then brought together to make a bond on contact. This bonding on contact is useful and the bond is flexible. It is not, however, very strong and it cannot be repositioned readily. Such glues are useful for sticking sheet materials such as plastic laminate and cork tiles. Some clear ones are used as multipurpose glues. Some have a toxic vapour. Trade names include Bostik 1, Bostik 3, Evo-Stik Impact, Loctite Clear, Power Fix, Thixofix, UHU and Unistik.

5 Latex adhesives These are natural rubber-based glues which can be used as contact adhesives or as conventional 'wet' adhesives. They are particularly useful for fabric, carpet and so on. They withstand washing but not dry-cleaning. Trade names include Copydex, Jiffybind and Surestick.

6 Vinyl adhesives These stick flexible vinyl (PVC) together to repair tears or fix two items together. The strong flexible bond makes them ideal for repairing rainwear, shower curtains and so on. Trade names include PVX and Vinylweld.

7 Superglue (cyanoacrylate adhesives) A good choice where a small, tight-fitting joint is required. It is not suitable for joining large areas, or for filling joints. It is quick-setting, expensive and it can stick your skin to itself or other objects. Trade names include Super Glue 3 and Ultrabond.

8 Epoxy resin adhesives The most versatile multipurpose adhesives. A resin and hardener are mixed together to form an adhesive which sets in a few minutes to several hours. The bond is strong and oil-, water- and heat-resistant. Trade names include Araldite, Araldite Rapid, Bostik 7 and Dunlop Epoxy.

9 Acrylic adhesives Similar to epoxy adhesives, but the resin can be applied to one surface and the hardener to the other. Expensive, but even oily surfaces can be joined together. Trade names include Hyperbond and Multi-bond.

10 Cellulose adhesives These are not very strong, but they are clear, quick-drying and are fairly heat- and water-proof. They are popular for repairing glass and crockery and in model-making. Trade names include Durofix and Samson C110.

11 Glue gun An effective general-purpose glue for heat-proof materials. An adhesive stick is melted in the chamber of the gun and is squeezed out by a trigger mechanism. The glue – white or clear – sets in about a minute.

12 Glue stick A non-toxic, solid adhesive in a lipstick-type dispenser. It is easy to wash off skin and clothes. It is used for card or paper. Trade names include Pritt Stick and UHU Stic.

Uses of adhesives

Type of adhesive	Purpose	Ceiling tiles	China	Fabrics	Floor tiles	General	Glass	Laminates	Leather	Metal	Paper/card	Rigid plastics	Vinyl sheet	Wood
Natural glue														
PVA			•	•					•	•	•			•
Urea-formaldehyde														•
Contact				•					•	•	•			
Latex		•		•					•	•				
Vinyl													•	
Superglue						•								
Epoxy						•								
Acrylic						•								
Cellulose			•	•			•	•						•
Glue gun						•								
Glue stick											•			

SHELVING
Putting up shelving is a relatively easy DIY job. It provides immediate results in terms of increased storage space and the attractive presentation of decorative items.

Types of shelving

There are two main types of shelving:
- fixed shelves, which are not adjustable; and
- shelving systems, which are adjustable.

Support Whether fixed or adjustable, shelves are supported in two ways:
- wall-mounted; or
- side-mounted.

Shelves for very heavy loads, such as large books, need to be both wall- and side-mounted.

Fixed shelving

L-shaped bracket (a) Inexpensive and practical, the bracket should be only slightly shorter than the width of the shelf.

Wooden batten (b) This cannot be used by itself – it is used as a reinforcement.

Wall mounting

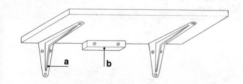

Bearer batten (c) The standard shelf method used to fix a shelf across an alcove involves the use of bearer battens. By adding an overhanging strip to the front of each shelf, you can hide the battens.

Side mounting

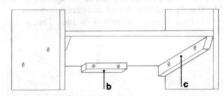

Adjustable shelving systems
Shelving systems, though generally more expensive, have the advantage of being adaptable to suit your changing circumstances.

1 Adjustable bracket Shelf-supporting brackets (**a**) are locked into notches in aluminium or wooden uprights (**b**).

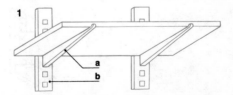

2 Plug Sometimes called studs or pegs, metal, plastic or wooden plugs are fitted into holes at the sides of the unit. The shelf rests on the plugs.

3 Invisible wire Here, the shelf has grooved ends which allow it to be slotted onto wire strips, attached to the sides of a cupboard or bookcase fitting.

4 Metal strip and stud Metal studs are inserted into slots in metal strips on the side of the unit. The shelf rests on the studs.

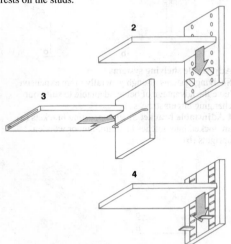

Mounting shelving

There are several factors to consider when mounting shelving.

Wall fixing This must be strong enough for the type of shelving used, the load on the shelving and the type of wall to which it will be fixed. Refer to the chart below to find the right fixing for your needs.

Choosing the correct wall fixing

Wall	Shelf use	
	Medium load (plate shelves)	Heavy load (book shelves)
Solid wall	Wall plug (use a cellular block plug if masonry behind is breeze block or aerated concrete block)	Wall anchor or No. 10 or 12 wall plug if masonry behind is brick or concrete
Lath and plaster wall	Toggle bolt or Screw into stud or joist behind plaster	Screw into stud or joist behind plaster

continued

Choosing the correct wall fixing (continued)

	Shelf use	
Wall	Medium load (plate shelves)	Heavy load (book shelves)
Drylined wall (plasterboard or masonry)	Wall plug (make sure plug goes at least 1 in into masonry behind plasterboard	Wall anchor (make sure wall anchor goes 1–2 in into masonry behind plasterboard
Partition wall*	Hollow-wall plug or Toggle bolt or Screw into stud of joist behind plasterboard	Screw into stud or joist behind plasterboard

* To find a wooden stud or joist behind the plaster, or plasterboard, tap the wall and listen for the hollow sound to change to a dull thud. In plasterboard, locate the rows of plasterboard nails using a magnet or hand metal detector.

Depth The shelves must be deep enough to support the items you wish them to carry. For example, a television set is quite deep and will probably need to be angled for viewing. An aquarium is both deep and very heavy.

Height The shelves for frequently-used items should be between waist and shoulder height.

Types of wall fixing
a wall plug
b wall anchor
c hollow wall plug
d spring toggle bolt

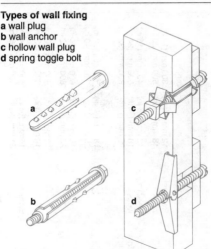

Shelf material This must provide sufficient strength at
the right price. Weaker shelf material will require more
support which may be unsightly. The additional fixings
may well cancel out any initial cost advantages. The
relative advantages and disadvantages of different types
of shelving material are summarized in the chart
overleaf.

Shelving materials: characteristics

Materials	Advantages	Disadvantages	Thickness of shelf	Maximum distance between shelf supports
Chipboard	Inexpensive	Relatively weak	12 mm (1/2 in) 18 mm (3/4 in)	300 mm (12 in) 500 mm (20 in)
Faced chipboard	Inexpensive – variety of colours and finishes available, including easy-clean	Relatively weak	12 mm (1/2 in) 18 mm (3/4 in) 25 mm (1 in)	400 mm (16 in) 600 mm (24 in) 800 mm (32 in)
Plywood	Strong and stiff		18 mm (3/4 in) 25 mm (1 in)	800 mm (32 in) 1000 mm (40 in)
Medium density fibreboard	Strong and stiff Suitable for painting		18 mm (3/4 in) 25 mm (1 in)	600 mm (24 in) 800 mm (32 in)
Blockboard	Strong and stiff		12 mm (1/2 in) 18 mm (3/4 in)	500 mm (20 in) 800 mm (32 in)
Finished wood	Strong and stiff Attractive	Expensive	15 mm (5/8 in) 21 mm (7/8 in)	600 mm (24 in) 900 mm (36 in)

LIGHTING
Electric lamps are available in two types:
tungsten-filament bulbs and fluorescent tubes.

Tungsten-filament bulbs

Clear bulbs should be used in enclosed fittings (as they are brighter), and pearl bulbs used where the naked eye is exposed to the light.

Fluorescent tubes

Fluorescent tubes are more efficient than tungsten-filament bulbs. For the same wattage, a tube gives off about four times as much light as a bulb.

Power (wattage)

Bulbs and tubes are both rated in watts (W); the wattage indicates how much electricity will be used when a lamp is on. It does not indicate how much light a lamp gives off, although it is obvious that a 40 W lamp is not as bright as a 60 W or a 100 W lamp.

When choosing bulbs of different wattage, bear in mind that certain rooms need more light than others.
Bedrooms, halls and stairways need medium lighting, and kitchens, work rooms and reading areas need bright light.

Types of light fitting

There are four main types of light fitting:
- ceiling-mounted (pendant or closed fitting);
- wall-mounted (various styles);
- concealed (including downlights and 'wall-washers'); and
- freestanding (table or standard lamps and uplights).

Types of bulb and tube

There are many different types of bulb and fluorescent light. Each has different uses and comes in different wattages with different caps. The charts on pp. 160–1 show what bulbs and tubes are available for different uses.

Tungsten-filament bulbs

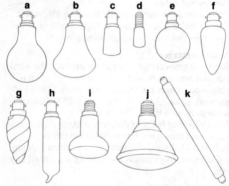

a standard pear shape
b mushroom
c pygmy
d appliance
e globe
f candle

g twisted candle
h pickwick
i reflector
j PAR (parabolic aluminized reflector)
k striplight

Bulb cap types

a bayonet (BC) **b** edison screw (ES) **c** small bayonet (SBC) **d** small edison screw (SES)

Fluorescent tubes

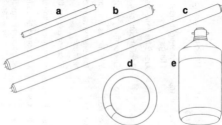

- **a** mini (15 mm [⅝ in] diameter)
- **b** standard (38 mm [1½ in] diameter)
- **c** slimline (25 mm [1 in] diameter)
- **d** circular (available in 2 sizes – 305 mm [12 in] or 406 mm [16 in])
- **e** fluorescent bulb

Fluorescent tube cap types

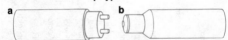

a bi-pin **b** double-ended tubular (DET)

Tungsten-filament bulbs and their uses

Type	Cap				Wattage	Use
	BC	ES	SBC	SES		
Pear	•	•			15, 25, 40, 60, 75, 100, 150	Basic household lighting
Mushroom	•				40, 60, 100, 150	Softer light, used for shallow fittings
Pygmy			•	•	15	Used for limited space
Appliance			•	•	15, 40	Appliances, sewing machines, etc.
Globe	•	•			25, 40, 60, 100	Decorative, for open display
Candle			•	•	25, 40, 60	Wall lights and chandeliers
Twisted candle			•	•	25, 40, 60	Decorative reproduction candle fittings
Pickwick			•		40	Flickering lamp fittings
Reflector		•	•		40, 60, 75, 100, 150	Spotlight or floodlight
PAR	•	•			80, 100, 150	Armoured glass for outside use
Striplight	Double-ended tubular				30, 60	Striplight fittings, offices, etc. Work only when horizontal

Fluorescent tubes and their uses

Type	Cap	Length (mm)	Wattage	Use
Standard 38 mm (1½ in)	Bi-pin	600, 900, 1200 1500, 1800, 2400	20, 30, 40 50, 75-85 125	Used mainly for workshops
Slimline 25 mm (1 in)	Bi-pin	460, 600, 900 1200, 1500	15, 18, 30 36, 50	Used in kitchens, bathrooms, etc.
Mini 15 mm (⁵/₈ in)	Mini bi-pin		4, 6, 8, 13	Worktop lights in kitchens – usually concealed
Circular 406 mm (16 in)	4-contact		40, 60	Decorative bathroom and kitchen lighting
Circular 305 mm (12 in)	4-contact		32	Decorative bathroom and kitchen lighting
Bulb	BC ES		9, 13, 18	Long-life replacement for for tungsten-filament bulb

5. In the garden

USEFUL MEASURES AND WEIGHTS
This section provides the various measures you
might need to help with your gardening. These
include length, area, volume, capacity, weight,
temperature, making dilutions and solutions, and other
useful calculations. There are conversion tables to aid
you in converting one unit to another. There are also
useful tips on using tools and other devices to estimate
measures.

LENGTH
Imperial units
Imperial units of length are measured in inches
(in), feet (ft), yards (yd), chains (ch), furlongs (fur) and
miles (mi).

$$1 \text{ ft} = 12 \text{ in}$$
$$1 \text{ yd} = 3 \text{ ft}$$
$$1 \text{ ch} = 22 \text{ yd}$$
$$1 \text{ fur} = 10 \text{ ch}$$
$$1 \text{ mi} = 8 \text{ fur or } 1760 \text{ yd}$$

Metric units
Metric units of length are measured in millimetres
(mm), centimetres (cm), metres (m) and kilometres
(km).

$$1 \text{ cm} = 10 \text{ mm}$$
$$1 \text{ m} = 100 \text{ cm}$$
$$1 \text{ km} = 1000 \text{ m}$$

Imperial to metric conversions
The main equivalents are as follows (use the table
below for further calculations):

$$1 \text{ in} = 25.4 \text{ mm or } 2.45 \text{ cm}$$
$$1 \text{ ft} = 0.3048 \text{ m}$$
$$1 \text{ yd} = 0.9144 \text{ m}$$

Imperial to metric conversion tables

**Inches, feet and yards
to millimetres, centimetres and metres**

Handy mm	Handy m	in	Exact mm	Exact m
25	0.025	1	25.4	0.025
50	–	2	50.8	–
75	–	3	76.2	–
100	–	4	101.6	–
125	–	5	127.0	–
150	–	6	152.4	–
175	–	7	177.8	–
200	–	8	203.2	–
225	–	9	228.6	–
250	0.25	10	254.0	0.254
275	0.28	11	279.4	0.279
300	0.30	12	304.8	0.305

Handy cm	Handy m	ft	Exact cm	Exact m
30	0.3	1	30.48	0.305
60	0.6	2	60.96	0.610
90	0.9	3	91.44	0.914

Handy cm	Handy m	yd	Exact cm	Exact m
90	0.9	1	91.44	0.914
910	9.1	10	914.40	9.144

Metric to imperial conversions
The main equivalents are as follows (use the table below for further calculations):

1 mm = 0.039 in
1 cm = 0.3937 in
1 m = 39.37 in or 3.281 ft

Metric to imperial conversion tables

Millimetres, centimetres and metres to inches, feet and yards

Handy in	Handy ft	mm	Exact in	Exact ft
0.04	0.003	1	0.039	0.003
0.20	0.015	5	0.197	0.016
0.40	0.030	10	0.394	0.033
Handy in	Handy ft	cm	Exact in	Exact ft
0.4	0.03	1	0.394	0.033
0.8	0.07	2	0.787	0.066
1.2	0.10	3	1.181	0.098
1.6	0.13	4	1.575	0.131
2.0	0.16	5	1.969	0.164
2.4	0.20	6	2.362	0.197
2.8	0.23	7	2.756	0.230
3.2	0.26	8	3.150	0.262
3.5	0.30	9	3.543	0.295
4.0	0.33	10	3.937	0.328
40.0	3.30	100	39.370	3.281
Handy ft	Handy yd	m	Exact ft	Exact yd
3.3	1.1	1	3.281	1.094
33.0	11.0	10	32.808	10.936

AREA
Imperial units
Imperial units of area are measured in square inches (sq in), square feet (sq ft), square yards (sq yd), acres and square miles (sq mi).

$$1 \text{ sq ft} = 144 \text{ sq in}$$
$$1 \text{ sq yd} = 9 \text{ sq ft}$$
$$1 \text{ acre} = 4840 \text{ sq yd}$$
$$1 \text{ sq mi} = 640 \text{ acres}$$

Metric units
Metric units of area are measured in square centimetres (sq cm), square metres (sq m), hectares (ha) and square kilometres (sq km).

$$1 \text{ sq m} = 10\,000 \text{ sq cm}$$
$$1 \text{ ha} = 10\,000 \text{ sq m}$$
$$1 \text{ sq km} = 100 \text{ ha}$$

Imperial to metric conversions
The main equivalents are as follows (use the table on the next page for further calculations):

$$1 \text{ sq in} = 645.2 \text{ square millimetres}$$
$$\text{(sq mm) or } 6.452 \text{ sq cm}$$
$$1 \text{ sq ft} = 0.093 \text{ sq m}$$
$$1 \text{ sq yd} = 0.836 \text{ sq m}$$
$$1 \text{ acre} = 0.405 \text{ ha}$$
$$1 \text{ sq mi} = 258.999 \text{ ha or } 2.590 \text{ sq km}$$

Imperial to metric conversions

Square inches, feet and yards to square centimetres and metres

Handy sq cm	Handy sq m	sq in	Exact sq cm	Exact sq m
6	–	1	6.452	–
13	–	2	12.903	–
19	–	3	19.355	–
26	–	4	25.806	–
32	–	5	32.258	–
39	–	6	38.710	–
77	–	12	77.420	–

Handy sq cm	Handy sq m	sq ft	Exact sq cm	Exact sq m
925	0.09	1	929.03	0.093
1860	0.19	2	1858.06	0.186
–	0.28	3	–	0.279
–	0.37	4	–	0.372
–	0.47	5	–	0.465
–	0.56	6	–	0.557
–	0.65	7	–	0.650
–	0.74	8	–	0.743
–	0.84	9	–	0.836

Handy sq cm	Handy sq m	sq yd	Exact sq cm	Exact sq m
8350	0.84	1	8361.27	0.836
–	1.67	2	–	1.672
–	2.51	3	–	2.508
–	3.35	4	–	3.344
–	4.18	5	–	4.181
–	5.02	6	–	5.017

Metric to imperial conversions

 Square centimetres and metres to square inches, feet and yards

Handy sq in	Handy sq ft	sq cm	Exact sq in	Exact sq ft
0.15	0.0011	1	0.155	0.00108
0.31	–	2	0.310	–
0.47	–	3	0.465	–
0.62	–	4	0.620	–
0.78	–	5	0.775	–
0.93	–	6	0.930	–
1.09	–	7	1.085	–
1.24	–	8	1.240	–
1.40	–	9	1.395	–
1.55	0.011	10	1.550	0.0108
15.50	0.110	100	15.500	0.1076

Handy sq ft	Handy sq yd	sq m	Exact sq ft	Exact sq yd
10.8	1.2	1	10.764	1.196
21.5	2.4	2	21.528	2.392
32.3	3.6	3	32.292	3.588
43.1	4.8	4	43.056	4.784
53.8	6.0	5	53.820	5.980
64.6	7.2	6	64.583	7.176
75.3	8.4	7	75.347	8.372
86.1	9.6	8	86.111	9.568
96.9	10.8	9	96.875	10.764
107.6	12.0	10	107.639	11.960
215.3	24.0	20	215.278	23.920
538.2	60.0	50	538.195	59.800
1076.4	120.0	100	1076.391	119.599

Metric to imperial conversions
The main equivalents are as follows (use the table on the previous page for further calculations):

$$1 \text{ sq mm} = 0.0016 \text{ sq in}$$
$$1 \text{ sq cm} = 0.155 \text{ sq in}$$
$$1 \text{ sq m} = 10.764 \text{ sq ft or } 1.196 \text{ sq yd}$$
$$1 \text{ ha} = 2.471 \text{ acres or } 0.00386 \text{ sq mi}$$
$$1 \text{ sq km} = 0.386 \text{ sq mi}$$

VOLUME

Imperial units

Imperial units of volume are measured in cubic inches (cu in), cubic feet (cu ft) and cubic yards (cu yd).

$$1 \text{ cu ft} = 1728 \text{ cu in}$$
$$1 \text{ cu yd} = 27 \text{ cu ft}$$

Metric units
Metric units of volume are measured in cubic centimetres (cu cm, also abbreviated as cc) and cubic metres (cu m).

$$1 \text{ cu m} = 1\ 000\ 000 \text{ cu cm}$$

Imperial to metric conversions
The main equivalents are as follows (use the table on the opposite page for further calculations):

$$1 \text{ cu in} = 16.387 \text{ cu cm}$$
$$1 \text{ cu ft} = 0.028 \text{ cu m}$$
$$1 \text{ cu yd} = 0.765 \text{ cu m}$$

Imperial to metric conversions

Cubic inches, feet and yards to cubic centimetres and metres

Handy cu cm	Handy cu m	cu in	Exact cu cm	Exact cu m
16	–	1	16.39	–
33	–	2	32.77	–
50	–	3	49.16	–
66	–	4	65.55	–
82	–	5	81.94	–
100	–	6	98.32	–
Handy cu cm	**Handy cu m**	**cu ft**	**Exact cu cm**	**Exact cu m**
28 317	0.03	1	28 316.8	0.028
–	0.06	2	–	0.057
–	0.09	3	–	0.085
–	0.11	4	–	0.113
–	0.14	5	–	0.142
–	0.17	6	–	0.170
–	0.20	7	–	0.198
–	0.23	8	–	0.227
–	0.26	9	–	0.255
–	0.28	10	–	0.283
–	0.57	20	–	0.566
–	0.77	27	–	0.765
Handy cu cm	**Handy cu m**	**cu yd**	**Exact cu cm**	**Exact cu m**
–	0.77	1	–	0.765
–	1.53	2	–	1.529
–	2.29	3	–	2.294
–	3.06	4	–	3.058

Metric to imperial conversions

Cubic centimetres and metres to cubic inches, feet and yards

Handy cu in	Handy cu ft	cu cm	Exact cu in	Exact cu ft
0.6	–	10	0.61	–
1.2	–	20	1.22	–
1.8	–	30	1.83	–
2.4	–	40	2.44	–
3.0	–	50	3.05	–
3.7	–	60	3.66	–
4.3	–	70	4.27	–
4.9	–	80	4.88	–
5.5	–	90	5.49	–
6.1	–	100	6.10	–
61.0	0.035	1000	61.02	0.035

Handy cu ft	Handy cu yd	cu m	Exact cu ft	Exact cu yd
35	1.3	1	35.32	1.31
71	2.6	2	70.63	2.62
106	3.9	3	105.94	3.92
141	5.2	4	141.26	5.23
177	6.5	5	176.57	6.54
212	7.8	6	211.89	7.85
247	9.2	7	247.20	9.16
283	10.5	8	282.52	10.46
318	11.8	9	317.83	11.77
353	13.1	10	353.15	13.08
706	26.2	20	706.29	26.16
1766	65.4	50	1765.73	65.40
3531	130.8	100	3531.47	130.80

Metric to imperial conversions
The main equivalents are as follows (use the table on the previous page for further calculations):

1 cu cm = 0.061 cu in
1 cu m = 35.315 cu ft or 1.308 cu yd

CAPACITY
Imperial units (UK)
Imperial units of capacity are measured in fluid ounces (fl oz), pints (pt), quarts (qt), gallons (gal) and bushels (bu).

1 pt = 20 fl oz
1 qt = 2 pt
1 gal = 8 pt or 4 qt
1 bu = 8 gal

Metric units
Metric units of capacity are measured in millilitres (ml), centilitres (cl) and litres (l).

1 cl = 10 ml
1 l = 100 cl or 1000 ml

Note:	1 ml = 1 cu cm
	1 l = 1000 cu cm
	1000 l = 1 cu m

Imperial (UK) to metric conversions

The main equivalents are as follows (use the table on p. 48 for further calculations):

$$1 \text{ fl oz} = 28.413 \text{ ml}$$
$$1 \text{ pt} = 0.568 \text{ l}$$
$$1 \text{ qt} = 1.137 \text{ l}$$
$$1 \text{ gal} = 4.546 \text{ l}$$

Metric to imperial (UK) conversions

The main equivalents are as follows (use the tables on p. 49 for further calculations):

$$1 \text{ ml} = 0.035 \text{ fl oz}$$
$$1 \text{ l} = 1.76 \text{ pt or } 0.880 \text{ qt}$$
$$\text{or } 0.220 \text{ gal}$$

Note:	
	$1 \text{ l} = 61.025 \text{ cu in}$
	$1 \text{ l} = 0.0353 \text{ cu ft}$
	$1 \text{ cu in} = 0.0164 \text{ l}$
	$1 \text{ cu ft} = 28.3169 \text{ l}$

 WEIGHT

Here, the words 'weight' and 'mass' can be taken to mean the same thing.

Imperial units (UK)

Imperial units of weight are measured in the 'avoirdupois system' using drams (dr), ounces (oz), pounds (lb), stones (st), quarters (qr), hundredweights (cwt) and tons.

$$1 \text{ oz} = 16 \text{ dr}$$
$$1 \text{ lb} = 16 \text{ oz}$$

1 st = 14 lb
1 qr = 2 st
1 cwt = 4 qr
1 ton = 20 cwt

Metric units

Metric units of weight are measured in milligrams (mg), grams (g), kilograms (kg) and metric tonnes (t).

1 g = 1000 mg
1 kg = 1000 g
1 t = 1000 kg

Note: A metric tonne is sometimes called a megagram (Mg).

Imperial (UK) to metric conversions

The main equivalents are as follows (use the tables on p. 43 for further calculations):

1 oz = 28.349 g
1 lb = 0.454 kg
1 st = 6.350 kg
1 ton = 1.016 t

Metric to imperial (UK) conversions

The main equivalents are as follows (use the tables on p. 44 for further calculations):

1 g = 0.035 oz
1 kg = 2.205 lb or 0.157 st
1 t = 0.9842 tons

TEMPERATURE
Units of temperature

Units of temperature are measured in Celsius (°C) or Fahrenheit (°F).

$$0 \text{ °C} = 32 \text{ °F}$$
$$0 \text{ °F} = -17.8 \text{ °C}$$

Celsius to Fahrenheit

°C	°F	°C	°F
−40	-40.0	−8	17.6
−30	-22.0	−7	19.4
−20	-4.0	−6	21.2
−19	-2.2	−5	23.0
−18	-0.4	−4	24.8
−17	1.4	−3	26.6
−16	3.2	−2	28.4
−15	5.0	−1	30.2
−14	6.8	0	32.0
−13	8.6	1	33.8
−12	10.4	2	35.6
−11	12.2	3	37.4
−10	14.0	4	39.2
−9	15.8	5	41.0

Converting Celsius and Fahrenheit
Use the following formulas to convert one
temperature unit system to another.

°C ⟶ °F (°C × 1.8) + 32
°F ⟶ °C (°F − 32) ÷ 1.8

°C	°F	°C	°F
6	42.8	20	68.0
7	44.6	21	69.8
8	46.4	22	71.6
9	48.2	23	73.4
10	50.0	24	75.2
11	51.8	25	77.0
12	53.6	26	78.8
13	55.4	27	80.6
14	57.2	28	82.4
15	59.0	29	84.2
16	60.8	30	86.0
17	62.6	40	104.0
18	64.4	50	122.0
19	66.2	60	140.0

OTHER MEASURES

Cups and spoonfuls (UK)

Often teaspoonfuls (tsp), dessertspoonfuls, tablespoonfuls (tbsp) and cups are used in measuring. Here are their equivalents in metric and imperial (UK) units.

$$1 \text{ tsp} = 5 \text{ ml or } 1/6 \text{ fl oz}$$
$$1 \text{ dessertspoon} = 10 \text{ ml or } 1/4 \text{ fl oz}$$
$$1 \text{ tbsp} = 18 \text{ ml or } 2/3 \text{ fl oz}$$
$$1 \text{ cup} = 0.2273 \text{ l or } 1/2 \text{ pt}$$

Water weights

The following are equivalents of water by weight.

$$1 \text{ gal} = 10 \text{ lb}$$
$$1 \text{ l} = 1 \text{ kg}$$

DILUTIONS AND SOLUTIONS

Dilutions

To dilute a concentrated fluid or solution, you add water or another thinning agent. The strength of a dilution is usually referred to as a percentage: that is, the ratio of the concentrate's weight to the thinning agent's.

- 10 cu cm of concentrate made up to 1 litre (1000 cu cm) with water makes a 1% dilution.
- 20 cu cm of concentrate made up to 1 litre with water makes a 2% dilution.

The tables opposite can be used to help calculate dilution percentages.

Metric and imperial (UK) dilutions

Metric dilutions
The quantity of concentrate needed is shown in black.

%	Quantity of water required					
	50 l	10 l	5 l	2 l	1 l	500 ml
1	500 ml	100 ml	50 ml	20 ml	10 ml	5 ml
2	1l	200 ml	100 ml	40 ml	20 ml	10 ml
3	1½ l	300 ml	150 ml	60 ml	30 ml	15 ml
4	2 l	400 ml	200 ml	80 ml	40 ml	20 ml
5	2½ l	500 ml	250 ml	100 ml	50 ml	25 ml
10	5 l	1 l	500 ml	200 ml	100 ml	50 ml

Imperial (UK) dilutions
The quantity of concentrate needed is shown in black.

%	Quantity of water required					
	100 gal	50 gal	10 gal	5 gal	1 gal	1 pt
1	1 gal	½ gal	16 fl oz	8 fl oz	1½ fl oz	¼ fl oz
2	2 gal	1 gal	1½ pt	16 fl oz	3 fl oz	⅝ fl oz
3	3 gal	1½ gal	2½ pt	1¼ pt	5 fl oz	⅝ fl oz
4	4 gal	2 gal	3⅓ pt	1½ pt	6 fl oz	¾ fl oz
5	5 gal	2½ gal	4 pt	2 pt	8 fl oz	1 fl oz
10	10 gal	5 gal	8 pt	4 pt	16 fl oz	2 fl oz

Solutions

To make a solution, you add a certain amount of a substance (usually a solid) to a fluid solvent (usually water). The strength of a solution is usually referred to as a percentage: that is, the ratio of the substance's weight to the solvent's.

- 1 kg of a substance dissolved in 100 litres (equivalent to 100 kg) of water makes a 1% solution.
- 2 kg of a substance dissolved in 100 litres of water makes a 2% solution.
- 1 lb of a substance dissolved in 10 gal (equivalent to 100 lb) of water makes a 1% solution.
- 2 lb of a substance dissolved in 10 gal of water makes a 2% solution.

The tables below and on the following page can be used to help calculate solution strengths.

Metric and imperial (UK) solutions

Metric solutions
The amount needed of the substance to be dissolved is shown in black.

%	Quantity of water required					
	100 l	50 l	10 l	5 l	1 l	500 ml
1	1 kg	500 g	100 g	50 g	10 g	5 g
2	2 kg	1 kg	200 g	100 g	20 g	10 g
3	3 kg	1.5 kg	300 g	150 g	30 g	15 g
4	4 kg	2 kg	400 g	200 g	40 g	20 g
5	5 kg	2.5 kg	500 g	250 g	50 g	25 g
10	10 kg	5 kg	1 kg	500 g	100 g	50 g

Imperial (UK) solutions
The amount needed of the substance to be dissolved is shown in black.

%	Quantity of water required					
	10 gal	5 gal	4 gal	3 gal	2 gal	1 gal
1	1 lb	8 oz	$6^3/_8$ oz	$4^3/_4$ oz	$3^1/_4$ oz	$1^5/_8$ oz
2	2 lb	1 lb	$12^3/_4$ oz	$9^5/_8$ oz	$6^3/_8$ oz	$3^1/_4$ oz
3	3 lb	$1^1/_2$ lb	$1^1/_4$ lb	$14^3/_8$ oz	$9^5/_8$ oz	$4^3/_4$ oz
4	4 lb	2 lb	$1^1/_2$ lb	$1^1/_4$ lb	$12^3/_4$ oz	$6^3/_8$ oz
5	5 lb	$2^1/_2$ lb	2 lb	$1^1/_2$ lb	1 lb	8 oz
10	10 lb	5 lb	4 lb	3 lb	2 lb	1 lb

USEFUL ESTIMATES FOR GARDENERS

In the garden or allotment, you won't always have a tape measure to hand to gauge and calculate distances, areas and volumes. Instead, use everyday garden implements and objects to estimate quantities.

Lengths
- A standard spade (**a**) or shovel is about 1 metre (m) or 1 yard (yd) long.
- The blade of a standard spade (**b**) is about 30 centimetres (cm) deep by 18 cm across, or 1 foot (ft) deep by 7 inches (in) across.

- A hand trowel (**c**) and a fork are both about 30 cm or 1 ft long.
- A standard rake (**d**) is about 1.5 m or 5 ft long.
- A broom handle (**e**) is normally 1.2 m or 4 ft long.

Areas

- Lay out a spade (**a**) and shovel (**b**) at right angles to one another. The area they enclose (**c**) is about 1 square metre (sq m) or 1 square yard (sq yd).
- Lay out a hand trowel (**d**) and fork (**e**) at right angles to one another. The area they enclose (**f**) is roughly 900 square centimetres (sq cm) or 1 square foot (sq ft).

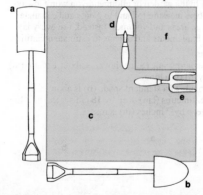

Volumes

- A standard wheelbarrow (**a**) or a dustbin (**b**), filled level, contains about 75 litres (l) or nearly 0.1 cubic metre (cu m). In imperial, this is about 17 gallons (gal), nearly 3 cubic feet (cu ft) or nearly ¹/₁₀ cubic yard (cu yd).
- A large water butt (**c**) contains roughly 280 litres or nearly 0.3 cu m. This is equivalent to 60 gal, 9 cu ft or 0.3 cu yd.
- A medium-sized water butt (**d**) contains roughly 100 litres or 0.1 cu m of water. This is equivalent to 22 gal, over 3 cu ft or ¹/₁₀ cu yd.
- A large watering can (**e**) contains roughly 9 litres or 2 gal of water. A medium-sized watering can (**f**) contains about 1¹/₂ gal or 6.5 litres of water.

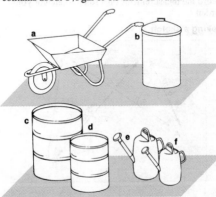

PLANNING A GARDEN
Whether you are taking over an existing garden, or starting from scratch with a new plot, it pays to plan your garden. Start by making a scale plan.

Making a scale plan for a square or rectangular plot
If your plot is square or rectangular, and the boundaries are at right angles or parallel to the house, follow the steps below.
1 Measure a fixed straight line with a tape measure: the back wall of the house (**a**), for example. Measure the length of the wall in metres (m), rounding to the nearest 10 centimetres (cm), or measure in yards (yd) and round to the nearest 3 inches (in).
2 Measure the boundaries with the tape measure and record the measurements on a rough sketch of your garden.

Making a sketch

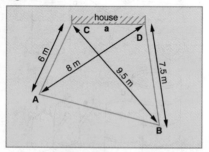

3 Transfer the measurements to graph paper, using a
simple scale such as one square equals 1 m. For
example, if the house wall measures 5 m long, it is
drawn as five squares on the graph paper (**b**). If you are
using imperial measurements, you can use a scale of
one square equals 4 feet (ft, **c**). If the wall is 20 ft long,
it is drawn as five squares long on the graph paper.

Planning on graph paper (one square = 1 m)

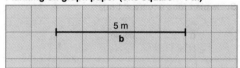

Planning on graph paper (one square = 4 ft)

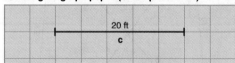

Making a scale plan for an irregular plot
If your plot is neither square nor rectangular, you will
need to measure two distances for each boundary
corner, such as **A** and **B** in the diagram on the previous
page.
1 Follow step **1** above.
2 Measure the distance from one corner of the house
(**C**) to a boundary corner (**A**).

3 Measure the distance from the other corner of the house (**D**) to **A**.

4 Continue in this way, measuring two distances for each boundary corner.

5 Record all the measurements on a rough sketch of your garden.

6 Transfer your measurements to graph paper, using a triangulation method to plot the boundaries.

Scale plan (one square = 1 m)

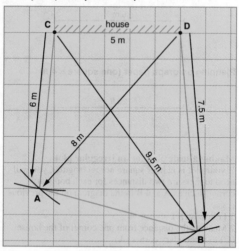

Triangulation method In the example shown on the previous page, boundary corner **A** is 6 m from house corner **C**, and 8 m from house corner **D**. On the graph paper, one square equals 1 m, so six squares equal 6 m and eight squares equal 8 m.

1 Use compasses to draw an arc the equivalent of six squares (6 m) from **C**.

2 Draw an arc eight squares (8 m) from **D**.

3 The two arcs cross at boundary corner **A**.

4 Continue to mark all the boundary corners in this way.

5 Join them with straight or curved lines corresponding to the sides of the plot.

Adding features to your plan

You can add features, such as the position of paths, the location of a vegetable plot, a pool and so on, by drawing them on your plan. When it comes to locating these areas in your garden, measure from a precise point on a boundary wall or from some other obvious feature in the garden.

Factors to consider There are many important factors to consider when deciding where to locate features in your garden. They include:

● aspect (which direction that part of the garden is
  `facing and so how much sun, wind and rain it
  receives);

● soil type (this will govern what plants can be grown)

● slope and drainage;

● distance from the house and boundaries (permanent
  structures over 1.8 m or 6 ft tall may require local
  planning permission); and

- costs (bear in mind the maintenance costs, not just
  the initial outlay).

Adding a pool to your plan

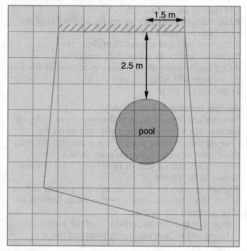

1.5 m

2.5 m

pool

Measuring areas of beds for plants
Easy mathematical equations for you to use when
working out areas of existing or new beds in your
garden start on the page opposite.

Rectangular beds

1 Multiply the height (**a**) by the
base (**b**). For example:

$$3 \text{ m} \times 4 \text{ m} = 12 \text{ sq m}$$

Triangular beds

1 Draw a line from one of the
angles to meet the side opposite
at right angles. Call this line the
height (**a**), and the side it
meets the base (**b**).
2 Multiply the height by the
base.
3 Divide by 2 to find the area.
For example:

$$3 \text{ m} \times 4 \text{ m} = 12 \text{ sq m}$$
$$12 \div 2 = 6 \text{ sq m}$$

Circular beds

1 Multiply the radius (**a**) of the
bed by itself.
2 Multiply the result by 22.
3 Divide this result by 7.
With a 3 m radius, for example:

$$3 \times 3 = 9$$
$$9 \times 22 = 198$$
$$198 \div 7 = \text{approx. } 28 \text{ sq m}$$

Oval beds

1 Multiply the extreme length
(**a**) by the extreme width (**b**).
2 Multiply the result by 11.
3 Divide this result by 14.
For example:

$$4 \text{ m} \times 2 \text{ m} = 8$$
$$8 \times 11 = 88$$
$$88 \div 14 = \text{approx. } 6 \text{ sq m}$$

Crescent bed

Estimate the area by
multiplying the extreme width
(**a**) by the extreme length (**b**).
For example:

$$4 \text{ m} \times 2 \text{ m} = 8 \text{ sq m}$$

Composite bed

1 Multiply the long length (**a**)
by the shorter height (**b**).
2 Multiply the rest of the
height (**c**) by the shorter length
(**d**).
3 Add the two results together.
For example:

$$4 \text{ m} \times 2 \text{ m} = 8 \text{ sq m}$$
$$2 \text{ m} \times 2 \text{ m} = 4 \text{ sq m}$$
$$8 + 4 = 12 \text{ sq m}$$

Marking out right angles in the garden

1 Mark out the corner of the angle with a peg or twig (**a**)
2 Run a 30 cm piece of string from peg (**a**) to a second peg (**b**).
3 Attach a 40 cm piece of string to peg (**a**) and a 50 cm piece of string to peg (**b**).
4 Where these meet, place a third peg (**c**), so creating a right angle.

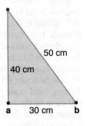

Marking out circles in the garden

1 Place a peg (**a**) where you want the centre of your circle.
2 Work out the radius of your circle, and cut some string just over this length.
3 Tie one end of the string to the peg (**a**) and the other to a marking stick (**b**).
4 Walk around the peg keeping the string taut while marking the circle on the ground.

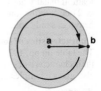

SOIL
Types of soil

Soils vary in density or bulk because of differences in texture and the amount of water they contain. Less dense soils occupy more space (volume) than denser soils of the same weight.

Sandy soil Sandy soil is the lightest available. It usually has a volume of about 1 cubic metre (cu m) to the metric tonne (t) or 35 cubic feet (cu ft) to the ton. Potting sand is slightly denser with a volume of 0.9 cu m to the tonne or 32 cu ft to the ton.

Loam Fibrous loam usually has a density of about 0.8 cu m to the tonne or 28 cu ft to the ton. Potting loam is similar.

Clay Clay soil is a much heavier type than sandy soil or loam. It usually has a density of 0.6 cu m to the tonne or 21 cu ft to the ton, and is approximately twice as heavy as sandy soil.

Characteristics of soil types

The table on pp. 192–193 shows the main soil types, their characteristics and methods of improving them. It also gives examples of plants that grow well in them.

Buying soil

Soil is generally sold in loads by volume, usually 1 cu m (1.3 cu yd or 35 cu ft) or by weight.

How much soil do you need?

To calculate the amount of soil you will need, work out the area to be filled and multiply it by the depth of soil required. For an illustration of how you should do this, see the worked example for calculating a quantity of topsoil on the page opposite.

Calculating how much topsoil you need
To calculate the amount of topsoil you will need to
cover an area of garden, follow the steps below.
1 Work out the area you want to cover with topsoil.
2 Decide on the depth of the topsoil required.
3 Multiply the area and the depth together to find the
amount of topsoil needed. For example, for a garden
that is 10 metres (m) by 6 m or 30 feet (ft) by 20 ft:

> area = 60 square metres (sq m)
> depth of topsoil required = 0.3 m (or 30 cm)
> so
> $60 \times 0.3 = 18$ cu m
> thus 18 cu m of topsoil will be needed

> or

> area = 600 square feet (sq ft)
> depth of topsoil required = 1 ft
> so
> $600 \times 1 = 600$ cu ft

> to convert cu ft to cu yd, divide cu ft by 27
> so
> $600 \div 27 = 22.2$ cu yd
> thus 22.2 cu yd of topsoil will be needed

If you are using the imperial system and you want
topsoil at a depth of less than 1 ft, follow the method
above, using 1 ft. Then multiply the answer by the
fraction of 1 ft that you want. For instance:

> 9 in = $^3/_4$ ft = 0.75 ft
> so
> 0.75×22.2 cu yd = 16.7 cu yd

Soil types and their characteristics

Soil type	Characteristics	Methods for improving soil	Plants that grow well
Sandy soil	Gritty. Does not compact into a ball when squeezed. Readily loses water and nutrients. Dries out quickly.	Dig in plenty of organic material (manure, compost etc.) and fertilizer in spring and autumn.	Achillea *Alyssum saxatile* Geranium Iris Lupin Veronica
Loam	The ideal medium, neither too light nor too heavy. Forms a ball when squeezed. Readily breaks into crumbs.	More a question of maintenance than improvement. Autumn digging and regular dressing of lime and fertilizer.	Most plants other than those which prefer damp or acid conditions.

Clay soil	Heavy to work. Waterlogged in winter and cracked in summer.	Break up by autumn digging and adding lime and organic material.	Aster Astilbe Campanula Hosta Primula Salvia
Chalky soil	Pale. Sticky when wet. Drains freely. Readily loses water and nutrients.	Dig in plenty of organic material and fertilize in spring and autumn.	Clematis Dianthus Gypsophila Hypericum Lathyrus Paeonia
Peaty soil	Dark. Rich in organic material. Spongy. Acidic.	Enhance drainage, add lime and dig in loam topsoil. Because it is rich in organic material, fertilizer does not need to be added.	Astilbe Hosta Lobelia Phlox Primula

VEGETABLES
Vegetable sowing and planting
Vegetables are sown, thinned out or planted out at certain distances. The spaces between them are dictated by the size to which they grow and the demands they make upon the soil. Some vegetables are sown in seed beds and later planted in the vegetable plot. Others are sown directly in the plot. Compare the instructions on the seed packet with your local growing conditions. This will help you to decide whether to sow the seeds in seed beds or to sow them directly into your plot.

Space, depth and season The charts on pp. 196–201 will help you to work out how far apart to sow seeds, the depth at which to plant them and when. They also show which vegetables need to be grown in seed beds and then transplanted to your vegetable plot.

Crop yields
Just a few seeds can generate a large weight of produce by the end of the growing season. The table opposite illustrates what sort of yield you can expect according to the size of your vegetable plot.

Seasonal differences
Spring in Cornwall arrives a month earlier than it does in Aberdeen. Therefore seasons, rather than months, have been given on the following pages as a guide for when to plant, sow and harvest your vegetable crops.

Vegetable crop yields

Vegetable	Yield kg		Yield lb/oz	
	1 sq m	1 m row	1 sq yd	1 ft row
Beans (broad)	1.2	0.75	2.3	8 oz
Beans (French)	0.7	0.375	1.5	4 oz
Beans (runner)	12	6	24	4 lb
Beetroot	2.5	1.3	5.5	14 oz
Broccoli	3	1.7	6	19 oz
Brussels sprouts	1	0.85	2	9 oz
Cabbage (spring)	2	1	4	11 oz
Cabbage (winter)	3.5	2.2	7	1.5 lb
Cauliflower	2.5	1.6	5	1 lb
Carrots (early)	1.5	0.45	3.75	5 oz
Carrots (main)	3	1.1	6.5	12 oz
Leeks	2.3	1.2	5	13 oz
Lettuce	12–14 heads	5–6.5 heads	10–13 heads	1.5–2 heads
Mushrooms	4.8	–	10	–
Onions	2.5	0.9	5.5	10 oz
Parsnips	2.3	1.2	5	13 oz
Peas	0.7	0.5	1.5	6 oz
Potatoes	2.5	2.2	5	1.5 lb
Spinach	1.5	0.45	3.75	5 oz
Swedes	2.7	1.3	6	14 oz
Turnips	2.7	1.3	6	14 oz

Vegetable sowing and planting guide

Vegetable	Seeds to grow 100 plants	Seeds or roots per 10 m/30 ft row	When to plant/ sow (plot)
Artichokes (globe)	–	10–16	mid spring
Artichokes (Jerusalem)	–	3.2 kg/ 7 lb	late winter
Asparagus	–	26–40	–
Beans (broad)	–	284 ml/ $1/2$ pt	early winter
Beans (French)	–	142 ml/ $1/4$ pt	early–mid spring
Beans (runner)	–	284 ml/ $1/2$ pt	late spring– early summer
Beetroot	–	7 g/ $1/4$ oz	mid spring– early summer
Broccoli	4.7 g/ $1/6$ oz	–	–
Brussels sprouts	3.5 g/ $1/8$ oz	–	–

Note: The seeds of some vegetables, such as beans and peas, are measured by capacity or volume (for

When to sow (seed beds)	When to transplant (to plot)	Distance between rows	Distance between plants/ to sow	Depth to plant/sow
–	–	90 cm/ 3 ft	90 cm/ 3 ft	5 cm/ 2 in
–	–	75 cm/ 2½ ft	35 cm/ 15 in	15 cm/ 6 in
mid spring	spring (following year)	90–120 cm/ 3–4 ft	35 cm/ 14 in	25 cm*/ 10 in
–	–	60 cm/ 2 ft	15 cm/ 6 in	2.5 cm/ 1 in
–	–	45 cm/ 1½ ft	20 cm/ 8 in	2.5 cm/ 1 in
–	–	2.5 m/ 8 ft	20 cm/ 8 in	2.5 cm/ 1 in
–	–	30 cm/ 1 ft	15–20cm/ 6–8 in	2.5 cm/ 1 in
early–late spring	late spring– mid summer	75 cm/ 2½ ft	60 cm/ 2 ft	1 cm/ ½ in
early–mid spring	late spring– early summer	75 cm/ 2½ ft	60 cm/ 2 ft	1 cm/ ½ in

continued

* Initially, roots should be covered only lightly with soil

example, millilitres [ml] or pints [pt] rather than weight).

Vegetable sowing and planting guide (continued)

Vegetable	Seeds to grow 100 plants	Seeds or roots per 10 m/30 ft row	When to plant/ sow (plot)
Cabbages (winter)	3.5 g/ 1/8 oz	–	–
Cabbages (spring)	3.5 g/ 1/8 oz	–	–
Carrots	–	7 g/ 1/4 oz	early spring– early summer
Cauliflower	3.5 g/ 1/8 oz	–	–
Celery (trench type)	1 g/ 1/32 oz	–	–
Cucumber	100/ seeds	–	–
Leeks	2 g/ 1/16 oz	–	–
Lettuce	–	3.5 g/ 1/8 oz	mid spring– late summer
Onions	–	4.7 g/ 1/6 oz	early spring
Parsley	–	7 g/ 1/4 oz	early spring– late summer
Parsnips	–	7 g/ 1/4 oz	late winter– early spring

When to sow (seed beds)	When to transplant (to plot)	Distance between rows	Distance between plants/ to sow	Depth to plant/sow
early–mid spring	late spring–mid summer	60 cm/ 2 ft	45 cm/ 18 in	1 cm/ 1/2 in
mid–late summer	early–mid autumn	30 cm/ 1 ft	15 cm/ 6 in	1 cm/ 1/2 in
–	–	15–20 cm/ 6–8 in	5–10 cm/ 2–4 in	0.5 cm/ 1/4 in
late winter–mid spring	late spring–early summer	75 cm/ 2 1/2 ft	60 cm/ 2 ft	1 cm/ 1/2 in
late winter–mid spring	early–mid summer	90 cm/ 3 ft	30 cm/ 1 ft	0.5 cm/ 1/4 in
mid–late spring	early summer	120 cm/ 4 ft	90 cm/ 3 ft	1 cm/ 1/2 in
early spring	early summer	45 cm/ 18 in	22 cm/ 9 in	0.5 cm/ 1/4 in
–	–	22–30 cm/ 9–12 in	15–22cm/ 6–9 in	1 cm/ 1/2 in
–	–	30 cm/ 1 ft	15 cm/ 6 in	1 cm/ 1/2 in
–	–	22 cm/ 9 in	13 cm/ 5 in	1 cm/ 1/2 in
–	–	45 cm/ 18 in	20 cm/ 8 in	2.5 cm/ 1 in

continued

Vegetable sowing and planting guide (continued)

Vegetable	Seeds to grow 100 plants	Seeds or roots per 10 m/30 ft row	When to plant/ sow (plot)
Peas	–	142 ml/ $1/4$ pt	early spring– early summer
Potatoes (early)	–	3.6 kg/ 8 lb	early spring
Potatoes (mid–late season)	–	3.2 kg/ 7 lb	mid spring
Radishes	–	14 g/ $1/2$ oz	early spring– late summer
Savoy cabbages	14 g/ $1/2$ oz	–	–
Spinach (winter)	–	7 g/ $1/4$ oz	late summer
Swedes	–	7 g/ $1/4$ oz	late spring– early summer
Tomatoes	7 g/ $1/4$ oz	–	–
Turnips	–	7 g/ $1/4$ oz	early spring– mid summer

When to sow (seed beds)	When to transplant (to plot)	Distance between rows	Distance between plants/ to sow	Depth to plant/sow
–	–	60–150cm/ 2–5 ft	7.5 cm/ 3 in	2.5 cm/ 1 in
–	–	75 cm/ 2¹/₂ ft	30 cm/ 1 ft	10–12.5 cm/ 4–5 in
–	–	90 cm/ 3 ft	35 cm/ 15 in	10–12.5 cm/ 4–5 in
–	–	15 cm/ 6 in	15 cm/ 6 in	0.5 cm/ ¹/₄ in
mid–late spring	early–late summer	60 cm/ 2 ft	45 cm/ 18 in	1 cm/ ¹/₂ in
–	–	30 cm/ 1 ft	15 cm/ 6 in	2.5 cm/ 1 in
–	–	35 cm/ 15 in	20 cm/ 8 in	1 cm/ ¹/₂ in
early spring (in greenhouse)	early summer	90 cm/ 3 ft	45 cm/ 18 in	0.5 cm/ ¹/₄ in
–	–	30–35cm/ 12–15 in	10–20 cm/ 4–8 in	1 cm/ ¹/₂ in

Seed storage

Seed producers grow rich on the seeds that are thrown away in half-empty packets. Don't throw them away! Properly stored in cool, dry conditions, most seeds will remain usable for a year or more. Use the chart below to check the life expectancy of your vegetable seeds.

Life expectancy of seeds

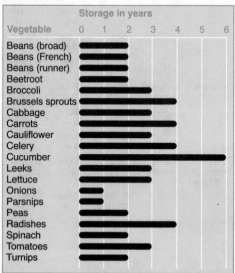

Vegetable	Storage in years
Beans (broad)	2
Beans (French)	2
Beans (runner)	2
Beetroot	2
Broccoli	3
Brussels sprouts	4
Cabbage	3
Carrots	3
Cauliflower	3
Celery	4
Cucumber	6
Leeks	3
Lettuce	3
Onions	1
Parsnips	1
Peas	2
Radishes	4
Spinach	2
Tomatoes	3
Turnips	2

Germination of seeds

Vegetable seeds take different times to germinate, depending upon conditions. The chart below gives approximate germination periods.

 Seed germination times

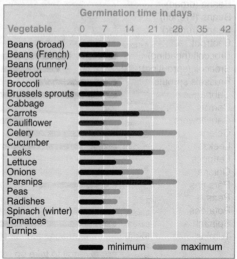

Germination time in days

Vegetable	0	7	14	21	28	35	42
Beans (broad)							
Beans (French)							
Beans (runner)							
Beetroot							
Broccoli							
Brussels sprouts							
Cabbage							
Carrots							
Cauliflower							
Celery							
Cucumber							
Leeks							
Lettuce							
Onions							
Parsnips							
Peas							
Radishes							
Spinach (winter)							
Tomatoes							
Turnips							

minimum ■ maximum

When to harvest vegetable crops

Depending upon the time of sowing or planting, the weather and the local growing conditions, the times when a crop is ready to be harvested will vary.

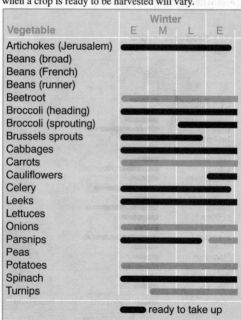

Vegetable	Winter			
	E	M	L	E
Artichokes (Jerusalem)	████████████████████
Beans (broad)				
Beans (French)				
Beans (runner)				
Beetroot	████
Broccoli (heading)	██████████
Broccoli (sprouting)			███████████
Brussels sprouts	███████████████
Cabbages	████████████████████
Carrots	████████████████████
Cauliflowers				███
Celery	████████████████
Leeks	████████████████████
Lettuces				
Onions	████████████████████
Parsnips	█████████████ ██████
Peas				
Potatoes	████████████████████
Spinach	████████████████████
Turnips			███████████

████ ready to take up

The chart below shows the times of the year when
vegetable crops are ready to be taken from the soil for
immediate use and also for storage and preservation.

Rotating vegetable crops

When growing vegetables, move each type of vegetable from bed to bed each year. This prevents the build-up of pests and diseases. It also prevents the soil in a bed from becoming seriously depleted of the nutrients favoured by a particular vegetable. The table below gives an example of possible crop rotation and suitable fertilizing jobs for one bed over three years.

 Three-year crop rotation plan

Year 1 **Brassicas** Cabbages, cauliflowers, Brussels sprouts, broccoli, kale, kohl rabi, swedes, turnips, radishes.

Dress soil with animal manure or compost and, later, with lime if necessary.

Year 2 **Root crops** Carrots, parsnips, turnips, beetroots, salsify, Jerusalem artichokes, potatoes.

No animal manure or compost with root crops. Also, do not add lime.

Year 3 **Other crops** Aubergines, beans, capsicums, celery, endive, leeks, marrows, onions, peas, spinach, sweet corn, tomatoes.

Add well-rotted manure or compost at digging time. Add lime only if soil is acid. Add fertilizers a few weeks before planting/sowing.

Methods of storing vegetables

Although most vegetables are best eaten fresh, storing them for use during the winter months is a very good idea. The table below gives different methods for storing various vegetables.

 Vegetable storage guide

Vegetable / Method	Clamp	Dry storage	Bottled	Pickled	Dried	Salted	Frozen	In ground
Beans (broad)					●	●	●	
Beans (French)					●	●	●	
Beans (runner)					●	●	●	
Beetroot	●	●		●			●	
Broccoli							●	
Brussels sprouts							●	
Carrots	●	●					●	
Cauliflower				●			●	
Cabbage (red)				●				
Leeks							●	●
Onions		●			●	●		
Parsnips							●	●
Peas					●		●	
Potatoes	●	●					●	
Spinach (summer)							●	
Tomatoes		●	●				●	
Turnips	●	●					●	

PLANTS AND PLANTING

Types of plant

Plants can be arranged in several categories: those that have a permanent structure and live for many years (trees and shrubs); those that grow during summer but die down in winter (herbaceous plants); or those that are raised from seeds each year (annuals and biennials). Annuals take one season in which to grow from seeds and to flower, but biennials require two.

Annuals and biennials

Annuals

Hardy annuals are sown outdoors in spring or early summer in the positions in which they are to grow and flower. In autumn, the plants die.

Half-hardy annuals are raised in a greenhouse in late winter or spring, the seedlings transferred to seed trays and the plants later planted outdoors once the risk of frost has passed.

Biennials

These are sown outdoors in seedbeds in late spring or early summer. In late summer or autumn, plants are transferred to their flowering positions, where they create a wealth of colour during the following year.

Herbaceous plants

These plants create a wealth of stems, leaves and flowers during summer, which die down to soil level

Herbaceous plants (continued)

in autumn and early winter. They remain as dormant plants during winter.

Bulbs, corms, rhizomes and tubers

These plants are specially adapted with roots or stems that store food. Some plants, such as daffodil bulbs, are relatively hardy and if planted in autumn survive outside during winter and produce flowers in spring. Others, such as dahlia tubers, are tender and planted only when there is no risk from frost.

Greenhouse perennials

These are tender plants which can only be grown in greenhouses in temperate regions.

 ## Trees and shrubs

These are woody plants with permanent stems and branches. Trees have only one stem (trunk) that connects the branches to the roots, while shrubs have several, creating a bush. Some are evergreen and retain their leaves. Deciduous types lose their leaves in autumn and develop fresh ones in spring. A few are semi-evergreen and lose only some of their leaves, depending on the severity of the weather.

Conifers

These range from prostrate, ground-hugging plants to those 30 m (100 ft) or more high. Most are evergreen, but some are deciduous.

Number of plants needed for herbaceous borders
When planning a border, you must consider how many
plants of different sizes you want. It is best to have
larger plants at the back and smaller ones near the front,
but the arrangement will also depend on the width of the
border. On average, four or five plants per square metre
or square yard are a good number to plant. As borders
increase in size, however, you can plant fewer plants. If
the herbaceous border is large enough, always plant
them in groups of three or five plants of the same type,
rather than singly. Position them to form a triangle,
rather than as a square or in a straight line. This is only a
rough guide based on average-sized herbaceous plants,
and the use of square units as a measure is not intended
to restrict the pattern of planting to squares. Smaller
plants can be planted much more closely together than
larger ones. Use the chart opposite to help plan the
number of plants (roughly) that you will need to fill
your border.

Plants for different soils and conditions
When buying plants for your garden, you should
consider the type of soil they are going to be grown in
(see pp. 192–193), and the weather conditions to which
they are going to be subjected. To gain an idea of what
would be suitable, look to see what plants are growing
in your neighbours' gardens, as they will probably have
the same type of soil as you.
Think about light, too, as some parts of your garden may
be in shade continuously and therefore not all plants will
grow in them. The charts on pp. 212–214 show some
plants that are suitable for certain conditions.

Estimating the number of plants for borders
The number of plants required are shown in black.

Width of border	Length of border				
	3 m (10 ft)	6 m (20 ft)	9 m (30 ft)	12 m (40 ft)	15 m (50 ft)
60 cm (2 ft)	12	24	36	48	60
90 cm (3 ft)	15	30	45	60	75
120cm (4 ft)	18	36	54	72	90
150 cm (5 ft)	20	40	60	80	100
180 cm (6 ft)	22	44	66	88	110
210 cm (7 ft)	24	48	72	96	120
240 cm (8 ft)	26	52	78	104	130
270 cm (9 ft)	27	54	81	108	135
300 cm (10 ft)	28	56	84	112	140

Plants for herbaceous borders

 Plants that grow well in shade

Anemone	Hosta
Aquilegia	Polygonum
Astilbe	Pulmonaria
Cimicifraga	Trillium
Convallaria	Trollius
(lily of the valley)	

 Plants that grow well in windy areas

Anemone	Polygonum
Centaurea	Potentilla
Bergenia	Scabious
Centranthus	Sedum
Geranium	Stachys

 Plants that grow well in dry situations

Achillea	Lupin
Anemone	Lychnis
Geranium	Nepeta (catmint)
Iris	Sedum
Kniphofia	Veronica

Plants that grow well in moist areas

Astilbe	Lysimachia
Caltha	Phlox
Hosta	Pulmonaria
Iris	Ranunculus
Lobelia cardinalis	Trollius

 Plants that grow well in clay soil

Aster	Hosta
Astilbe	Iris
Caltha	Polygonum
Campanula	Primula
Geranium	Salvia

 Plants that grow well in chalk and limestone soils

Anthemis	Filipendula
Artemisia	Gypsophila
Aster	Paeonia
Centaurea	Pyrethium
Dianthus (pink)	Scabious

**Five low-growing
herbaceous plants**

Alchemilla	Helleborus
Astilbe	Heuchera
Bergenia	

 **Five tall herbaceous
plants**

Aruncus	Ligularia
Crambe	Lupin
Delphinium	

Annual and biennial bedding plants

Annuals are plants which grow, flower and die over one
year; biennials do this over two years. Both are
commonly bought as bedding plants that will flower in
the garden. Match heights and colours for the desired
effect.

 **Planning guide
for annuals**

Name	Colour	Height cm/in
Ageratum (floss flower)	Mauve	15–30/6–12
Alyssum	White, pink, lilac	7–15/3–6
Antirrhinum (snapdragon)	White, yellow pink	15–90/6–36
		continued

Planning guide for annuals (continued)

Name	Colour	Height cm/in
Begonia semperflorens	White, pink, red	15–30/6–12
Cosmos	Yellow, red, orange	30–60/12–24
Gazania	Yellow, orange	22–37/9–15
Impatiens	Red, pink, white	15–60/6–24
Lobelia	Blue	15–20/6–8
Marigolds	Yellow, orange, crimson	15–60/6–24
Matthiola (stocks)	White, pink, red, purple	30–45/12–18
Nemesia	Various	15–45/6–18
Nicotiana	White, pink	30–90/12–36
Papaver rhoeas (field poppy)	Scarlet	45–60/18–24
Petunia	White, blue	30–45/12–18
Phlox	White, scarlet, purple, etc.	15–45/6–18
Salpiglossis	Various	45–60/18–24
Salvia	Scarlet, purple	15–60/6–24
Tagetes	Orange, yellow	15–22/6–9
Ursinia	Orange	30–35/12–15
Verbena	Scarlet, blue, carmine, white	23–30/9–12
Viola (pansy)	Pink, purple, orange, yellow	15–22/6–9

Perennial bedding plants

Perennials are plants which live three or more years.
The stems and leaves usually die back in the winter, but
the roots remain alive. The plants grow new shoots and
leaves each spring. To plan your garden using
perennials, match height, colour and flowering period
for the desired effect.

**Planning guide for herbaceous
perennial plants**

Name	Colour	Height cm/in	Flowering period
Acanthus	Orange, pink	90–120/36–48	MSu
Alstroemeria	Orange, pink	90/36	MSu
Aster	Various	15–180/6–72	LSu–MAu
Astilbe	White to red	30–90/12–36	MSu–LSu
Campanula	Blue, white	15–120/6–48	LSp–MSu
Carnations	Various	60/24	MSu
Delphiniums	Blue, white	90–180/36–72	ESu–MSu
Euphorbia	Yellow, orange	30–60/12–24	MSp–LSp
Geranium	Blue, red	30–90/12–36	ESu–EAu
Gypsophila paniculata	White	60–90/24–36	MSu–LSu
Helianthus	Yellow	150/60	MSu–MAu
Kniphofia	Yellow to red	60–240/24–96	ESu–MAu

continued

E = early	Sp = spring
M = middle	Su = summer
L = late	Au = autumn

Planning guide for herbaceous perennials (continued)

Name	Colour	Height cm/in	Flowering period
Liatris	Purple	22–30/9–12	MSu–LSu
Limonium	Blue, pink	30–60/12–24	LSu–EAu
Lupinus	Various	90–120/36–48	ESu
Lychnis	Red	30–90/12–36	MSu–LSu
Lysimachia punctata	Yellow	60–90/24–36	ESu–LSu
Lythrum salicaria (purple loosestrife)	Red-purple	60–120/24–48	ESu–EAu
Macleaya (plume poppy)	Pearly-white	150–240/60–96	
Monarda didyma (bee balm)	Scarlet	30–90/12–36	ESu–EAu
Paeonia	White to red	60–90/24–36	LSp–ESu
Phlox	White to red	30–120/12–48	MSu–EAu
Platycodon (balloon flower)	Light blue	30–60/12–24	ESu–LSu
Pulmonaria	Blue, red	15–45/6–18	ESp–MSp
Pyrethrum	White to red	90/36	ESu
Rodgersia	White, pink	90/36	MSu–LSu
Rudbeckia	Yellow	60–200/24–79	MSu–EAu
Salvia superba	Blue	45–90/18–36	MSu–EAu

E = early	Sp = spring
M = middle	Su = summer
L = late	Au = autumn

Bulb planting

Plants grown from bulbs, corms or tubers flower at various times, from spring through to autumn. The table below shows plants that flower in spring or in summer and when to plant them.

 Bulb-planting guide for spring- and summer-flowering plants

Plant	Spring/ summer	When to plant
Achimenes (nut orchid)	Summer	Pot in early spring. Plant out after last frost
Allium (flowering onion)	Summer Spring	Early spring Late autumn
Amaryllis	Summer Spring	May Pot in early Dec. Plant out in May
Anemone (wind flower)	Spring	Oct
Begonia	Summer	Feb/Mar in dark room. Move into light room when shoots appear, and 6 weeks later plant out
Calla	Summer	Pot in Oct
Chionodoxa (glory-of-the-snow)	Spring	Autumn
Convallaria (lily of the valley)	Spring	Late summer
Crocus	Spring	Oct/early Nov

continued

Bulb-planting guide (continued)

Plant	Spring/summer	When to plant
Daffodil	Spring	Sep/Oct
Dahlia	Summer	Spring (after last frosts)
Fritillaria	Spring	Autumn
Galanthus (snowdrop)	Spring	Sep/Oct
Gladiolus	Summer	Spring up to early Jul
Hemerocallis (daylily)	Summer	Early spring to late summer
Hyacinth	Spring	Oct
Iris (dwarf)	Spring	Oct/Nov
Iris (tall)	Summer	Oct
Leucojum (snowflake)	Spring	Autumn
Lilium candidum	Summer	Sep
Lilium (hybrids)	Summer	Oct/Nov
Lycoris (spider lily)	Summer	Aug
Narcissus	Spring	Sep/Oct
Scilla (squill and bluebells)	Spring	Oct/Nov
Tuberose	Summer	May
Tulip	Spring	Late Oct/early Nov

Plants for rock gardens and walls

The chart below gives a variety of plants you can plant in rock gardens, with their heights, colours, time of flowering and whether to position them in open, shady, or sunny positions.

 Rock garden and wall plant guide

Plant	Height cm/in
Aethionema X ('Warley Rose')	15/6
Alyssum saxatile ('Citrinum')	15/6
Androsace sempervivoides (rock jasmine)	5/2
Arenaria purpurascens	5/2
Asperula caespitosa	5/2
Bellis perennis (daisy)	2.5–10/1–4
Campanula portenschlagiana (bell flower)	10/4
Dianthus caesius (Cheddar pink)	22/9
Erinus alpinus ('Dr Hanele')	7.5/3
Iris lacustris	12.5/5
Saxifraga burseriana	2.5/1

Colour	Times of flowering	Position
Pink	Summer	Sunny
Yellow	Late spring	Sunny
Pink	Late spring	Sunny
Lilac	Spring	Sunny
Pink	Summer	Open
Pink or white	Summer	Open
Blue	Almost continuous	Sunny or shady
Pink	Summer	Open
Carmine	Late spring	Sunny
Various	Spring	Sunny
Yellow	Spring	Open

Indoor plants
The chart below gives a variety of plants you can grow indoors, with their heights, colours and some remarks on how to keep them.

 Indoor plant guide

Plant	Height cm/in
Begonia rex (rex begonia)	30/12
Chlorophytum elatum (spider plant)	30–37/12–15
Cissus antarctica (kangaroo vine)	Climbing plant
Coleus hybrids (flame flower)	30–60/12–24
Hedera (ivy)	Climbing plant
Peperomia caperata	7–25/3–10
Sansevieria trifasciata (mother-in-law's tongue)	45–90/18–36
Tradescantia pallida	30–37/12–15
Callisia elegans	30/12
Tradescantia fluminensis (wandering Jew)	Trailing plant

Colour/foliage	Remarks
Patterns of green, cream, red, purple	Keep away from direct sunlight
Green and white	Easily propagated and grown
Green	Easy to train up cane stakes
Various	In summer, can plant outdoors
Green or variegated	In summer, keep out of direct sunlight
Dark green	
Swordlike in shape	Can cope with periods of dryness
Purple	
Green and white	Easy to grow
Green, white or yellow variegated	Use in hanging baskets

TREES AND SHRUBS

Trees

When trees grow, they can become tall and broad, so you need to plan ahead. How tall will a tree become? How broad? Use the table below to help you decide which trees to plant where. Assume that the roots underground spread at least as far as the branches above.

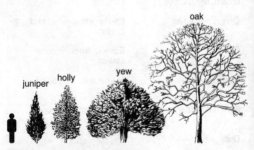

 Trees – height and spread after 15 years

Name	Height m/ft	Spread m/ft
Juniper	3/10	1/3
Holly	3/10	1.3/4
Yew	3.6/12	5/16
Oak	7.6/25	6.4/21

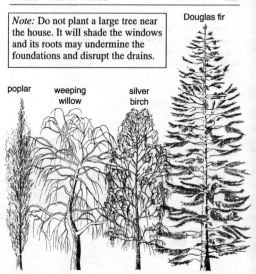

Note: Do not plant a large tree near the house. It will shade the windows and its roots may undermine the foundations and disrupt the drains.

Name	Height m/ft	Spread m/ft
Poplar	9/30	2/6.5
Weeping willow	9/30	6.6/22
Silver birch	9/30	4/13
Douglas fir	12/40	5.3/17

Shrubs

When planting shrubs decide on the effect you want to create. Do you want isolated shrubs or do you want to create a hedge? How tall and wide do you want each shrub to be? Use the table below to help you decide which shrubs to plant where.

Cotoneaster horizontalis

Daphne

Camellia

Spiraea japonica

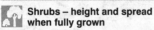

Shrubs – height and spread when fully grown

Name	Height m/ft	Spread m/ft
Cotoneaster horizontalis	1.2/4	2/6.5
Daphne	1.5/5	1.5/5
Camellia	1.5/5	1.3/4
Spiraea japonica	0.9–1.5/3–5	1.2–1.8/4–6
Berberis*	2/6.5	2.5/8
Ribes	2.4/8	2/6.5
Buddleia davidii	2.4–3/8–10	1.8–2.4/6–8

Note: Some families of shrub have members with very different growth rates and shapes. Check with the supplier before purchasing a particular variety.

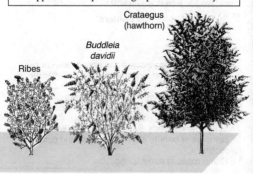

Crataegus (hawthorn)

Buddleia davidii

Ribes

Name	Height m/ft	Spread m/ft
Crataegus (hawthorn)*	4.6/15	3.6/12
Prunus 'Ukon'	4.6–6/15–20	5.5–10.7/18–35
Magnolia	6/20	7/23
Rhododendron	9/30	12/40

Those marked * are suitable for hedges.

CARING FOR PLOTS AND BORDERS
Throughout the year your plots and borders
will need care and attention. The following
chart lists the jobs that you will need to do by season.

 **Care of plots and borders
by season**

Spring

- Begin sowing vegetables and annual flowers as soon as the soil is workable and warm (after the last frost).
- Plant summer-flowering bulbs and corms.
- Prune spring-flowering shrubs and climbers immediately after flowering.
- Mulch permanently planted areas with well-rotted compost or bark to suppress weeds and conserve moisture.
- Prune roses in early spring.

Summer

- Water soil at the beginning or end of the day.
- Regularly feed vegetables and flowering plants with liquid fertilizer.
- Continue sowing vegetables for continuity of cropping.
- Add activator to the compost heap to aid rapid breakdown of plant refuse.
- Dead-head roses and other early summer-flowering plants.

continued

Care of plots and borders by season (continued)

Autumn

- Sow broad beans for an early crop the following year.
- Plant spring-flowering bulbs and bedding plants.
- Cut back the stems of roses and other tall shrubby plants.
- Trees, shrubs and fruit bushes can be replanted as soon as their leaves fall.
- Lift, move and divide large clumps of herbaceous perennials.
- Plant spring-flowering bulbs (except tulips) as soon as they become available.
- Check the pH of the vegetable plot soil and apply lime if it is acidic.
- Begin rough winter digging and fork in organic matter.

Winter

- Complete winter digging before the soil freezes.
- Make firm plants loosened by the heaving of frozen soil.
- Towards the end of winter, place cloches over vegetable beds to warm soil for first sowings in March.

LAWNS

Turf sizes and shapes

Turfs are usually sold in two sizes,
and come with different qualities of grass.

- Mostly, they are cut in 30-centimetre (cm) or 1-foot (ft) wide by 1-metre (m) or 3-ft long strips, but these can vary in depth from one place to another, and do not make perfectly even lawns.
- Sometimes they are cut in 30 cm (1 ft) squares, which lay much more evenly and are better for surfaces such as bowling greens.

Available quantities of turf

Turfs are sold by the hundred squares or strips:

- 100 strips (30 cm × 1 m) will cover 30 square metres (sq m) or about 33⅓ square yards (sq yd).
- 100 squares (30 cm × 30 cm) will cover 9 sq m or about 11 sq yd.

Calculating how many turfs you need

To calculate how many strips or squares of turf you would need for your lawn, divide the area of one strip or square into the area that needs to be covered.

> one square = 900 sq cm or 0.09 sq m
> one square = 1 sq ft or 0.11 sq yd
> one strip = 3000 sq cm or 0.3 sq m
> one strip = 3.3 sq ft or 0.37 sq yd

For example, for a lawn of 30 sq m:

number of squares of turf required = 30 ÷ 0.09 = 333

number of strips of turf required = 30 ÷ 0.3 = 100

Laying turfs

When laying turfs, it is a good idea to have some loose soil handy to fill in and level off uneven places under the turf.

1 Lay the turfs in rows and make sure you keep them straight as you go.

2 When laying the second row, stagger the joints (a) to prevent the turfs from lifting up.

3 Beat the turfs down with the back of a spade to bring them into close contact with the soil (b).

4 If the surface is uneven, carefully lift the turf and add or remove soil to level it off.

5 Brush soil into any gaps between the turfs.

6 After a few weeks, apply weedkiller (c) if necessary.

7 Once the grass has grown to 3–4 cm (1¹/₂–2 in) high, your new lawn can be cut.

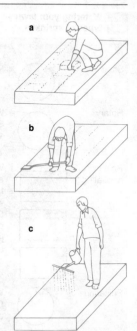

Watering your lawn – types of sprinkler

Sprinkler		Uses/area watered
Static		• Waters a circular area.
Rotary		• Waters a circular area. • Some are adjustable to water only sectors.
Rain or oscillating	**a** **b** **c**	• Waters a rectangular area (**a**). • Most are adjustable to water the left or right (**b**). • Can be adjusted to produce shorter ranging jets and so water a narrow rectangle of lawn (**c**).
Pulsating		• Waters a circular area. • Can be adjusted to water only sectors.
Mobile sprinkler		• These can cover a large area.

Seasonal care for your lawn

Use the chart below to help plan the care your lawn will
need throughout the year.

 **Lawn care
by season**

Spring
- Apply weedkiller/feed dressing to lawn.
- Repair damaged lawn edges.
- Start lawn mowing with cutters set high.
- Sow or turf new lawns.

Summer
- Lower blade setting on lawn mower and
  try to cut lawn twice a week.
- Keep lawn well watered and fertilized,
  possibly with a selective weedkiller.

Autumn
- Rake lawn/remove leaves soon after falling.
- Apply mosskiller, rake out dead moss and
  spike the lawn.
- Apply winter lawn fertilizer.
- Sow or turf new lawns.

Winter
- Clear twigs and other fallen debris.
- Check, oil and service lawn mowers and
  other mechanical equipment.

PATHS AND PAVING

The following information and chart will help you to estimate how much of a paving material you will require to make a path or terrace.

Paving slabs

Paving slabs can be bought in various forms, though the most common are rectangular and crazy paving.

Crazy paving Crazy paving is sold in two grades:
- thin: 2–4 cm or ³/₄–1¹/₂ in; or
- thick: 4–6 cm or 1¹/₂–2¹/₂ in.

It is sold in metric tonnes (t) or tons.
- 1 tonne of 'thin' paving will cover 11.5–13 square metres (sq m).
- 1 ton of 'thin' paving will cover 14–16 square yards (sq yd).
- 1 tonne of 'thick' paving will cover 6.5–7.5 sq m.
- 1 ton of 'thick' paving will cover 8–9 sq yd.

Rectangular paving This is also sold in two grades, so similar weights of this to crazy paving cover similar areas.

Gravel

Gravel is sold by the cubic metre (cu m) or cubic yard (cu yd)

A gravel path is usually between 5 and 7.5 centimetres (cm) or 2 and 3 inches (in) thick.
- 1 cu m of gravel will cover 12.5–20 sq m.
- 1 cu yd of gravel will cover 12–18 sq yd.

Paving quantities required for making a 3-m (10-ft) long path

The number of bricks, and weights of the other materials needed, are shown in black.

Type (thickness)	Width					
	60 cm (2 ft)		90 cm (3 ft)		180 cm (6 ft)	
Bricks						
• flat	71		107		214	
• on edge	107		160		320	
Crazy paving	kg	cwt	kg	cwt	kg	cwt
• (2–4 cm/³/₄–1¹/₂ in)	150	3	225	4¹/₂	450	9
• (4–6 cm/1¹/₂–2¹/₂ in)	260	5¹/₄	400	8	800	16
York slabs	200	4	300	6	600	12
Gravel						
• (5 cm/2 in)	190	3³/₄	250	5	500	10
• (7.5 cm/3 in)	250	5	375	7¹/₂	750	15
Concrete (5 cm/2 in)						
• gravel	150	3	225	4¹/₂	450	9
• sand	50	1	75	1¹/₂	150	3
• cement	50	1	75	1¹/₂	150	3
Concrete (7.5 cm/3 in)						
• gravel	225	4¹/₂	300	6	650	13
• sand	75	1¹/₂	100	2	210	4¹/₄
• cement	75	1¹/₂	100	2	210	4¹/₄

GREENHOUSES
Seasonal jobs in the greenhouse
Throughout the year plan the use of your greenhouse for best effect. The chart below should help you.

Jobs in the greenhouse by season

Spring
- Ensure that there is adequate shading and ventilation before temperatures start to rise.
- Sow major spring- and summer-flowering bedding plants.
- Plant hanging baskets.
- In late spring, move bedding plants from greenhouse to garden in preparation for major summer planting.

Summer
- Move hanging baskets outside.
- Fumigate the greenhouse every 14 days against pest.
- Ventilate well and damp down floors and stage daily to maintain humidity.
- Regularly feed and water plants.

Autumn
- Move frost-tender plants into the greenhouse.

continued

Jobs in the greenhouse by season (continued)

- Remove summer shading from greenhouse.
- Sow annuals for spring flowering.

Winter
- Sow seeds in heated propagators for plants with a long growing season.
- Order seeds through mail-order suppliers.
- Take root cuttings.
- Wash and disinfect pots, seed trays and other used equipment.
- Clean, tidy, wash and disinfect the greenhouse.
- Water plants sparingly.
- Store bulbs and tubers.
- Check and remove or treat diseased plants.

Calculating the volume of a greenhouse or lean-to

To calculate the volume of your greenhouse, follow the steps below.

1 Multiply the width (**a**) by the length (**b**).

2 Multiply the result by the height to halfway between the eaves and the ridge (**c**).

 or

FERTILIZERS

Adding fertilizer to soil replaces the nitrogen, phosphorus and potassium which it has lost. Adding compost or farmyard manure provides organic matter (or humus). The addition of these substances to the soil can both improve its physical properties and help it to retain nutrients already present.

How and when to use fertilizers

Using the wrong fertilizer, or using the right fertilizer at the wrong time, will not produce the desired result, and may be harmful. This table shows what type of fertilizer to use, during which season.

How and when to use fertilizers

Fertilizer	Main nutrients	When to apply	Main uses
Blood (dried)	Nitrogen (fast-acting)	Spring	Leafy growth; used to encourage quick growth in spring and summer
Bonemeal	Phosphorus (slow-acting)	Prior to planting or sowing	Encourages root growth
			continued

How and when to use fertilizers (continued)

Fertilizer	Main nutrients	When to apply	Main uses
Compound fertilizer (NPK)	Nitrogen, phosphorus, potassium (fast-acting)	Spring, summer	General garden use (including lawns)
Lime*	Liberates nutrients from acid soil	Autumn	Reduces soil acidity
Nitro-chalk	Nitrogen (fast-acting)	Spring	Reduces soil acidity and encourages rapid growth
Sulphate of ammonia	Nitrogen (fast-acting)	Spring	Fast-acting
Sulphate of potash	Potassium (fast-acting)	Spring, summer	General garden use
Super-phosphate	Phosphate (fast-acting)	Spring	General garden use
*Do not add with manure or compost			

Fertilizer quantities

Too little fertilizer, or using the wrong fertilizer, will not produce the desired result. Adding too much fertilizer is not only wasteful, it can be positively harmful. It can cause leaf 'burn', and the excess nutrients in water draining from your land may be harmful to nearby rivers and lakes. Use this table to make sure you use the correct quantities of fertilizer. Most fertilizers are sold as solids (in powdered or granular form).

 Quantities of fertilizer required

Fertilizer	Amount per sq m (sq yd)	Form
Blood (dried)	30–60 g (1–2 oz)	In water
Bonemeal	60–110 g (2–4 oz)	As solid
Compound fertilizer (NPK)	110 g (4 oz)	As solid or in water
Lime	225–450 g ($\frac{1}{2}$–1 lb)	As solid
Nitro-chalk	15–30 g ($\frac{1}{2}$–1 oz)	As solid
Sulphate of ammonia	15–30 g ($\frac{1}{2}$–1 oz)	As solid or in water
Sulphate of potash	15–30 g ($\frac{1}{2}$–1 oz)	As solid or in water
Super-phosphate	30–60 g (1–2 oz)	As solid or in water

Mixing fertilizer solutions

Instructions for mixing liquid fertilizers, weedkillers or other solutions often state the concentration required in grams (g) per litre (l) or ounces (oz) per gallon (gal). Use this table or the imperial one overleaf for calculating the correct quantity of fertilizer to add to different volumes of water.

Mixing fertilizer solutions: metric measures

The weight (in g) of the substance required is shown in black.

Quantity of water (litres)	Concentration of solution (g per litre)				
	5 g/l	7.5 g/l	10 g/l	15 g/l	25 g/l
1	5	7.5	10	15	25
2	10	15	20	30	50
5	25	37.5	50	75	125
10	50	75	100	150	250
50	250	375	500	750	1250
100	500	750	1000	1500	2500

Mixing fertilizer solutions: imperial measures

The weight (in lb/oz) of the substance required is shown in black.

Quantity of water (gal)	Concentration of solution (oz per gal)									
	1/4 oz/ gal		1/2 oz/ gal		1 oz/ gal		2 oz/ gal		5 oz/ gal	
	lb	oz	lb	oz	lb	oz	lb	oz	lb	oz
1		1/4		1/2		1		2		5
2		1/2		1		2		4		10
5		1 1/4		2 1/2		5		10	1	9
10		2 1/2		5		10	1	4	3	2
50		12 1/2	1	9	3	2	6	4	15	10
100	1	9	3	2	6	4	12	8	31	4

WEEDKILLERS
How and when to use weedkillers

The best way to clear weeds, and to keep them clear, is by yearly digging and regular hoeing. Getting to weeds before they flower, and digging out all root fragments of perennial types, greatly reduces the problem. Mulching with leaf litter or bark helps to prevent them from reappearing.

If you feel you have to use a weedkiller (for example, if you have to clear a plot quickly and easily, or you wish to keep a path or lawn weed free), the table on the following pages summarizes the information you need to know.

Types of weedkiller

Herbicide This term, meaning 'plant-killer', is a more accurate term than 'weedkiller'. By choosing the method, time and place to apply a particular weedkiller, you can ensure that weeds, rather than your wanted plants, are killed.

Total herbicides These kill almost all kinds of plants.

Selective herbicides These kill certain kinds of plants.

Contact herbicides These kill those parts of the plant with which they have direct contact.

Systemic or translocated herbicides These enter the plant by its leaves or roots and are then transported to all parts of the plant.

Residual herbicides These remain active in the soil for long periods and prevent the growth of seedlings or small plants.

How and when to use weedkillers

Name	Type	Use	Method of application/ precautions	Dangers
2,4-D Dicamba MCPA Dichlorprop Mecoprop	Sel, S	On lawns.	Spraying or watering. Prevent drift to other parts of the garden.	Harmful to most plants other than grass. Most of these lawn applications are harmful to fish.
Dalapon	Sel, S	Removing grasses around fruit bushes or trees or in vacant ground.	Spraying or sprinkling.	In large quantities, harmful to broad-leaved plants.

Diquat Paraquat	Tot, C	Removing weeds and other plants by direct contact.	Spraying or as a gel. Avoid contact with the stems and leaves of wanted plants.	Harmful to humans and animals. Use disposable gloves and avoid inhalation.
Glyphosate	Tot, S	For rapid removal of weeds from specific locations.	Spraying or as a gel. It does not persist in the soil and works best during periods of active growth.	Harmful to all plants.

continued

C = contact herbicide
S = systemic or translocated herbicide
Sel = selective herbicide
Tot = total herbicide

How and when to use weedkillers (continued)

Name	Type	Use	Method of application/ precautions	Dangers
Simazine	Tot, R	For keeping paths, drives clear. In small quantities can clear weeds from around specific plants.	Spraying or sprinkling.	In large quantities, harmful to all plants.
Sodium chlorate	Tot, S, R	For clearing ground and keeping paths, drives, etc. clear.	Spraying or watering. It may be carried to other parts of the garden through the soil water.	Inflammable when dry. Kills all plants. In dry weather or heavy soils, it may remain active for six months or more.

R = residual herbicide   S = systemic or translocated herbicide   Tot = total herbicide

PESTS AND PESTICIDES

The table below shows how three types of pesticides work, and what they are used for.

Types of pesticide

Types	Use against	How they work
Insect-contact pesticides	Sap-sucking insects, e.g. greenfly and capsid	By hitting and killing the insect with a forceful spray
Leaf-contact pesticides	Plant-chewing insects, e.g. caterpillars	By coating the insects' source of food
Systemic pesticides	Sap-sucking insects and small caterpillars	Enter the plant and are transported through it to poison the insect feeders

Garden and greenhouse pests

The following chart shows a few of the many pests that attack plants in gardens and greenhouses (they are not drawn to scale). Refer to the table on p. 250 to find out which insecticide to use for these pests and others.

1 Aphids (greenfly) attack a wide range of plants. They suck sap, causing distortion, and transmit viruses.

2 Cabbage rootfly maggots eat roots of brassicas, such as cabbages, cauliflowers and Brussels sprouts. Infested plants wilt and, in dry weather, usually die.

3 Capsid bugs infest ornamental plants, bushes and fruit trees. They suck sap, causing distortion and puckering of young leaves and damage to buds.

4 Caterpillars are the larvae of butterflies and moths. They chew leaves, stems and buds. Additionally, they foul vegetable crops, often making them inedible.

5 Cutworms are the larvae of several moths. They chew the stems of seedlings and young plants at ground level, causing them to collapse.

6 Flea beetles chew small, circular holes in leaves of plants such as turnips, cabbages and wallflowers.

7 Leafhoppers are related to aphids and suck sap, causing distortion. They jump when disturbed. Young leafhoppers feed on the undersides of leaves.

8 Leaf miners are the larvae of moths and flies. They burrow into the leaves of plants, causing tunnels which eventually spread and become blotches. There is often damage to chrysanthemums.

9 Red spider mites are minute spider-like creatures with eight legs. There are several different types, which attack plants in greenhouses and orchards.

10 Thrips (thunderflies) suck sap and cause silvery mottling and distortion of leaves and flowers.

11 Weevils are beetle-like, with long snouts. The larvae and adults feed on roots, stems, leaves, flowers, corms, tubers and fruits.

12 Whiteflies resemble minute, white moths. Young whiteflies feed on the undersides of leaves, causing distortion and making plants sticky.

13 Wireworms are the larvae of click beetles. They live in soil, feeding on roots and tubers and plant stems.

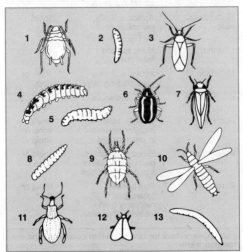

Common pesticides and their uses

Pesticide	Pests combated	Apply as
Cypermethrin	Ants, earwigs, woodlice, other crawling and creeping pests	liquid
Fenitrothion	Pea moth, raspberry beetle, codling moth, other foliar pests	liquid
Horticultural soaps	Aphids, whitefly, red spider mite, leafhoppers, scale	liquid
Lindane	Many soil and foliar pests	dust
Malathion	Aphids and other plant-sucking pests	liquid or dust
Metaldehyde	Slugs and snails	pellets or liquid
Permethrin	Whitefly, caterpillars, many other pests in greenhouses	smoke cone or liquid
Pyrethrins	Broad spectrum of pests, especially on fruit and vegetables	liquid or dust
Rotenone	Flea beetles, caterpillars, raspberry beetle, weevils, other pests	liquid or dust

Note: Always check the label to confirm a chemical's use and the pests it kills.

Index

COLLINS GEM

Other Gem titles that may interest you include:

Gem Ready Reference
A unique compendium of information from the
world of weights and measures **£2.99**

Gem Ready Reckoner
Easy-to-use tables provide the answers to a wide
range of calculations **£2.99**

Gem Encyclopedia
Over 600 topic-based pages and 750 two-colour
diagrams covering everything from the Roman
empire to the population of Monaco **£5.99**

Gem Fact File
A handy, quick-reference guide to thousands of
difficult-to-remember or difficult-to-find facts,
covering geography, language, science, the arts,
religion, sport and society **£3.50**

Gem First Aid
A guide to first-aid treatment for a wide range of
both life-threatening conditions and common,
everyday ailments and injuries **£3.50**